16+ ENGLISH

Other English books for schools and colleges from
Stanley Thornes (Publishers) Ltd

FOCAL ENGLISH by A T Jones, A D Burgen, I W Hosker
ELEPHANTS ARE DAINTY BIRDS by R K Sadler, T A Hayllar, C J Powell
EVERYDAY ENGLISH by K Mathias
GUIDE TO BETTER SPELLING by A M Burt
TESTS IN ENGLISH FOR OVERSEAS STUDENTS by M Kassem

16+ ENGLISH

An English Coursebook for Students in
Colleges of Further Education,
Sixth Form Colleges and the 'New Sixth'

M Baber MA(Cantab)

Senior Lecturer
Shirecliffe College, Sheffield

Stanley Thornes (Publishers) Ltd

Stanley Thornes (Publishers) Ltd
Educa House
Old Station Drive
off Leckhampton Road
CHELTENHAM GL53 0DN

First published 1982

British Library Cataloguing in Publication Data

Baber, Michael
    Sixteen-plus English.
    1. English language — Grammar — 1950-
    I. Title
    428   Pt1112

    ISBN 0-85950-325-9

Typeset by Tech-Set, Brewery Lane, Felling, Tyne and Wear
Printed and bound in Great Britain at The Pitman Press, Bath

Contents

PREFACE   vii

ACKNOWLEDGEMENTS   viii

1. WRITING AND TALKING — ARE THERE TWO ENGLISH
    LANGUAGES?   1
    Is this your problem?   1
    Regional accents and dialects   2
    Slang, catch phrases and colloquial expressions   4
    Idioms   5
    Written and spoken English: basic differences   6

2. EFFECTIVE TALKING   11
    Giving a talk   11
    Interviews   17
    Group discussion   21

3. WOULD YOU BE SO KIND? VARIETIES OF TONE AND
    REGISTER   31
    Levels of formality   31
    Which levels to use when — and why   33
    Tone and register   37

4. WHAT DOES YOUR WRITING TELL PEOPLE?   41
    Handwriting   41
    Punctuation: does it really matter?   43
    Spelling: how important is it?   50
    Vocabulary: how many words do you know?   51
    Who are you writing to?   55
    Why are you writing anyway?   56

5. TYPES OF WRITING   57
    Informative writing   57
    Descriptive writing   65
    Narrative writing   70
    Dialogue   78

Persuasive writing: arguing a case   80
Short stories   88
Reviews   92
Business letters   101
Business reports   109
Essays   112

6. STUDY SKILLS AND RESEARCH SKILLS   118
    What kind of student are you?   118
    Reading skills   121
    Using libraries   125
    Surveys and questionnaires   127
    Projects   131

7. COMPREHENSION, SUMMARY AND TAKING NOTES   136
    What's your problem?   136
    Why 'in your own words'?   142
    What can comprehensions test?   143
    Evaluating a comprehension   144
    DIY comprehension   146
    Exam comprehensions: a survival guide   153
    Summary and precis writing   153
    Taking notes   158
    Some final comprehension practice   161
    The end?   165

Preface

This book aims to provide a full one-year course in English for students taking O-Level English Language at 16 +, especially those in the 'New Sixth' and in Sixth Form, Tertiary or Further Education Colleges. It would also be particularly relevant for students following Mode 3 style courses.

For convenience the material is arranged by subject, and in an order that seemed logical to me — but the format is in no sense prescriptive. Please feel free to use the material in any order that seems useful to you, and feel free to use material in other ways than the chapter headings might indicate. You may find, for instance, that the whole book involves 'comprehension' and not just the chapter so labelled.

To try to ensure that the book will actually work in the classroom most of the material was pretested across a range of 16 + school and college classes before being included. I therefore owe a great deal to the students and colleagues concerned, especially those at Southport Technical College and Barking College of Technology. Singling out individuals is always difficult but I would like to say a special thank you to Ian Farrington for co-editing a prototype Work Book with me at Southport, and for allowing me to use material from it, and to Maureen Collins for pretesting material so extensively at Lutterworth High School and for providing such useful and encouraging comments.

M BABER

Acknowledgements

The author and publishers are grateful to the following for permission to reproduce previously published material:

Macmillan Ltd, for extracts from *Varieties of English* by G L Brook and *Juno and the Paycock* by Sean O'Casey

OUP (New York) and University of California Press, for an extract from *A Practical Guide to The Teaching of English as a Second or Foreign Language* by W M Rivers and M S Temperley

Sweet & Maxwell Ltd, for an extract from *A Casebook on Criminal Law* (3rd Edn) three cases by D W Elliott & J C Wood

Thomas Cook for an extract from their holiday brochure

NAL Times Mirror, for an extract from *Measure for Measure* by William Shakespeare

The TV Times and *London Express News*, for extracts from 'Reading Beyond the Lines' by Ed Stewart and 'Sun Tan Preparations'

The Guardian, for an extract from 'Wronged by how you Write'

The Associated Examining Board, for an extract from the *1978 O-Level Chief Examiners' Report on English Language*

The Joint Matriculation Board, for an extract from the *1978 Examiners' Report on A-Level English Literature*

Faber & Faber Ltd, for an extract from *WODWO* by Ted Hughes

J Garnet Miller Ltd, for an extract from *Carmilla* by Sheridan LeFanu

Granada Publishing Ltd, for extracts from *Standard Literacy Tests* by Hunter Diack and *The Female Eunuch* by Germaine Greer

CPC (United Kindom) Ltd, for the use of the instruction on the label of the Mazola Pure Corn Oil bottle

Longman Group Ltd, for extracts from *Investigating English Style* by D Crystal & D Davy and *Teaching English as a Second Language* by J A Bright & G P McGregor

The Institute of Physics, for an extract from *Journal of Physics* D: *Applied Physics* (1978)

Lake District Mountain Accidents Association, for an extract from *Fell Walkers Read This*

W H Allen & Co Ltd, for an extract from *Uncle Ernest* by Allan Sillitoe

National Extension College, MSC and BBC, for an extract from the *Roadshow Guide*

Heinemann Educational Books, for an extract from *A Walk in the Night* by Alex La Guma

Hutchinson Publishers Ltd, for an extract from *The Dear Green Place* by Archie Hind

Weidenfeld (Publishers) Ltd, for extracts from *The Garrick Year* and *The Millstone* by Margaret Drabble

Penguin Books Ltd, for extracts from *The Companion* by Y Yevtushenko, *Housewife* by Ann Oakley and *His and Hers* by Joy Groombridge

Rondor Music (London) Ltd, for extracts from *Show Some Emotion* by Joan Armatrading

The Hamlyn Publishing Group Ltd, for an extract from *Myths and Legends of Africa* by Margret Carey

William Heinemann and The Bodley Head, for an extract from *The Power and The Glory* by Graham Greene

A M Heath & Co, for extracts from *Catch-22* by Joseph Heller and *The Country Girls* by Edna O'Brien

The estate of the late George Orwell and Martin Secker & Warburg Ltd, for an extract from *A Hanging* by George Orwell

Jonathan Cape Ltd, for extracts from *Darkness at Noon* by Arthur Koestler and *The Wasteland* by Alan Paton

A P Watt Ltd, for an extract from *Selected Short Stories* by H G Wells

Python (Monty) Pictures Ltd, for an extract from *Monty Python's Previous Record*

Consumers' Association, for an extract from *Buying and Renting TV*

Department of Education and Science, for an extract from *Notes on the Setting and Marking of Examinations in English for National Certificates and Diplomas in Business Studies*

Robert Westall, for an extract from *The Vacuum and The Myth*

East African Publishing House, for an extract from *Song of Ocol* by Okot p'Bitek

The Times, for an extract from their 'May Day Editorial' (6 May 1980)

Southport Visiter, for an extract from 'Recalling the years of change for all'

Thorsons Publishers Ltd, for an extract from *Communicating Effectively* by Beryl Williams (first published 1977)

The Sunday Times, for extracts from 'Fashion in Faces' by Peter Quennell, 'On the Scent' by Hazel Meyrick Evans, 'In Search of Beauty' by Alex Finner, 'The Nile File' by George Perry and 'Cavemen'

ASA Ltd, for an extract from *Spare the Rules, Spoil the Children*

The New Standard, for an extract from 'Tongue tied by too much TV'

Arts Alive Merseyside, for an extract from *The Lonesome Road* by Chris Malone

David & Charles (Holdings) Ltd, for an extract from *Getting Through* by Godfrey Howard

Radio Times, for extracts from 'Help' by Bob Smyth, 'The Future of Television' and 'Life and Death'

Pan Books Ltd, for an extract from *Airport International* by Brian Moynahan

The Observer, for an extract from 'I am Well — Who are You?'

Cassell Ltd, for extracts from *The Necklace* and *Who Knows?* by Guy de Maupassant

William Collins Sons & Co Ltd, for an extract from *Food for Free* by Richard Mabey

Methuen & Co Ltd, for an extract from *Wordswork* edited by R Eagleson

Dominion Press Ltd, for an extract from *Why Go To Polytechnic?* by R B Taylor

Committee of Directors of Polytechnics, for an extract from 'Down to the Sea' from *Focus on Polytechnics* (Autumn 1979)

Souvenir Press, for an extract from *The Peter Principle* by L J Peter and R Hull

Manchester Evening News, for an extract from the 'Sex Trap Murder Case'

Joan Littlewood Productions Ltd, for an extract from *Oh What a Lovely War* © 1965

We have tried to contact all copyright holders. Should anyone inadvertently have been overlooked we apologise and will include full acknowledgement in future editions.

Writing and talking

Are there two English languages?

Do you ever make mistakes when you're writing, and then wonder why? And do you wonder because no one tells you you're wrong when you *talk* like that?

If so, you're not on your own. The differences between talking and writing cause problems for a lot of people — often because they don't realise just what the differences are.

Let's start with an exaggerated example. How many mistakes can you find in this letter — and how many can you trace back to differences between writing and talking?

> 101 Rotten Row,
> Mould on the Marsh.
> Wednesday.
>
> Dear Travel Company,
>
> Cor blimey – what a nerve! That holiday you just give us were a right washout. I mean we could tell the day we arrived. Everyone looked as miserable as sin and the cutlery were filthy and there weren't no tea and our Phyllis had no sheets on her bed for a week and the bread rolls were just stuck on filthy sacks on the floor. I mean what do you think you're playing at? That were a two hundred quid holiday. And our Fred woke up one morning just crawling with ants and with all that drilling for water in the back yard there wasn't no rest either. And what happened to the plane, that's what I want to know. So come on then cough up – its time you lot was sorted out.
>
> Yours affectionately,
>
> Mavis.

Now let's look at the differences between writing and talking in more detail.

Regional accents and dialects

(a) **Judge:** What are these oonty-toomps you keep mentioning?

Witness: What be oonty-toomps? They be the toomps the oonts make.

Judge: But what are oonts?

Witness: Why, them as make the toomps.

(extract from a court case in Worcester: in case your're still wondering, *oonty-toomps* are molehills)

(b) ... the men of Gilead said unto him, 'Art thou an Ephraimite?' If he said 'Nay', then they said unto him, 'Say now Shibboleth'; and he said 'Sibboleth', for he could not frame to pronounce it right. Then they took him and slew him.

(Judges 7:5, Authorised Version)

(c) During the Second World War many children were evacuated from London to the countryside, to be safe from German bombing. A teacher was asked whether it had affected the way the children spoke. His reply was, 'Not particularly. They went away saying "we was" and they came back saying "us be".'

(d) Australian tourists frequently refer to their patron saint, Emma Chizzit (how much is it?).

These examples show some of the differences between written and spoken English. They are mainly the result of dialect. Dialect isn't just a question of pronunciation and accent, as in (b) and (d). It is also a question of vocabulary (words peculiar to that area like *oonty toomps*) and grammar (*we was* or *us be* instead of 'we were').

In general, dialect isn't used when writing (or rather one particular dialect, variously called standard English, BBC English etc., is used). For one thing it probably wouldn't be easily understood outside the area where the dialect is used.

Exercise

1.1

1) Find an outline map of the British Isles. On it fill in as many regional dialects as you know of.

2) Then prepare a table giving, *for each dialect*, an example of

(i) pronunciation (e.g. the strong pronunciation of *ng*, for instance in the word 'hanging' in Liverpool)

(ii) grammar (e.g. I *be* instead of 'I am' in Somerset)

(iii) vocabulary (e.g. *brass* for 'money' in Yorkshire)

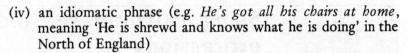

(iv) an idiomatic phrase (e.g. *He's got all his chairs at home*, meaning 'He is shrewd and knows what he is doing' in the North of England)

which differs from standard English, and thus from the English you would write.

3) Then prepare an extended list of such examples from the speech of your own area.

4) Prepare a list of famous people who speak, if not in a regional dialect, at least with a distinct regional accent.

5) Briefly explain the differences between

(i) accent and dialect

(ii) dialect and standard English.

To give you a little help with these questions, here are a few more examples containing dialect speech:

(e) There's wee-er laddies than me that goes round there and start tossing stones at the laddies round there. They usually get battered fae them if they get caught . . .

(f) I says, I can remember when I used to shove a bairn about in a pram for a tanner a week. Lots of money a tanner then a week. And I says, I've been pushed for money ever since, so they divn't come back. Put them out on the road. Wey lad, get away, go on. Aye, he says, for a tanner. By, you can do a lot with a tanner.

(g) She was er an Australian, I think yeh, and she was here that long waiting for a place that I took her in for three weeks . . . him and her . . . and they were . . . she was a great person . . . I was made up because I didn't take no rent off her . . .

(h) . . . this was before I married, see and, well this was the night, see, when I met my husband and erm you know they was like the b — the fellow was buying us drinks and that, see, and er my friend and her sister, oh, she say, we don't want to go with them . . .

(i) and there was Harry, his car or something had went wrong and he was . . . says I, Harry, what are you doing here, says I, you could be shot, says I . . .

Note. Some aspects of the above — the sentences started but not finished, the use of *er* and *erm*, the repetition (*says I . . . says I . . .*) and so on — are not really characteristics of dialect. They are, as we shall see, typical of people speaking rather than writing.

So far I have suggested that speaking in dialect (provided the person you are speaking to is from the same area and understands) is fine — but that when writing you should use standard English.

Dialect is only one part of the problem, though. Let us look at some other variations.

3

Slang, catchphrases and colloquial expressions

Slang

It is natural that many of the slang words current today have to do with drug addiction. Since it is illegal to sell or possess certain drugs, those who traffic in them have good reason to develop their own secret language, and the people who take drugs are often those who would in any case make free use of slang. We thus have *grass* for hashish, and *mainline* (to take narcotics intravenously) *to push* (to peddle drugs) and *trip* to describe the state of hallucination induced by a drug. A man under the influence of a drug is *high* or *turned on* or *stoned*. If he becomes dependent on drugs he is said to be *hooked*. A drug that is not habit-forming is said to be *soft* while the drug known as LSD is, among others, described as *acid*.

(from *Varieties of English* by G L Brook)

Slang is more difficult to write about — because it comes and goes so quickly. The drug-culture slang of the late 60s and early 70s seen above will perhaps seem rather old-fashioned to you by now.

Exercise 1.2

1) Do you agree with what the passage above says about *why* people use slang? If you don't, give your own suggestions.

2) Make a list of current slang. Then translate each word or phrase into more standard English.

Catch phrases

Radio, television and films all provide catch phrases. Rather like slang we use them in speech for a while and then move on to new catch phrases. Advertising jingles, disc jockeys' catch phrases, and memorable lines from films or plays all provide material. Can you think of any examples?

Colloquial expressions

These are expressions people use when speaking — perhaps to liven up the conversation — but which are usually too vague, imprecise or exaggerated to be used in writing. In any case they have normally been used so often that they have lost their effect. Examples include: *loads*, *tons*, and *millions* for 'a large quantity'; or *fantastic*, *dead great*, *really great* for 'good'. What examples of colloquial expressions can you think of?

Idioms

When we talk we sometimes also use idoms. In case you're wondering what an idiom is, look at the statements below. They all contain idioms.

There wasn't room to swing a cat

Use a bit of elbow grease

Stop beating about the bush

Let's get down to brass tacks

I'm turning over a new leaf

You've bitten off more than you can chew there

You're a dark horse and no mistake

Dead as a doornail!

Don't go off the deep end

It's time you stood on your own two feet

That's your funeral

It's the thin end of the wedge.

Exercise 1.3

1) Can you say what an idiom is?

2) The list above gives twelve examples. Can you match that by giving twelve of your own?

3) Suggest why idioms are better used when speaking rather than writing.

So, spoken English may contain dialect, slang, idiomatic and colloquial expressions and catch phrases — all of which should normally be *avoided* in writing (unless you are actually quoting people talking).

But the differences between written and spoken English go deeper than this. To help you see the differences let us look at two extracts.

(a) **From a tape recording of a conversation**

Listen — these two girls that I know that fly have been flying exactly three years — and they've been all over — and they — Rome, Athens, Greece, Egypt — every place — on their passes you know — they take two three weeks off and its just fabulous — and this one girl met this guy in — uh — in Egypt — and she just fell madly in love with him — well it was so funny and now she can't — she had to come home in two weeks — that's one thing because she can't you know be with him or anything — Egypt — I mean how far away can you get — kind of a bad problem — she's supposed to be going back in August — he's sent her tickets — a ticket — her and her sister — for them to go back.

(*b*)   **As the above might appear in ordinary written English**

Two stewardesses that I know have been flying exactly two years. They've been to all sorts of places. They can occasionally take two or three weeks off. When they do, they go everywhere — Athens, Rome, Egypt — on their passes. It's a wonderful experience for them. One of the girls met a man in Egypt and fell in love with him. But the difficulty was that she had to come home in two weeks. Now she can't be with him, because Egypt is too far away. This is a real problem for her. She's supposed to go back in August. The man has even sent tickets for her and her sister so that they can go back.

(from *A Practical Guide to the Teaching of English* by W M Rivers and M S Temperley)

What differences can you see?

Written and spoken English: basic differences

A   As the first extract shows, normal speech does not follow normal sentence patterns. We have chunks of meaning — separated by pauses — not neat capital letter/subject/predicate/full stop/new sentence as in written English. Conversational speech is full of hesitations, self-interruptions and false starts, e.g.

this guy in — uh — Egypt,

and they — Rome, Athens, Greece,

and now she can't — she had to come home.

B   There is no *necessary* connection between the way a word is spelt and the way it is pronounced. A short example would be the word *bow*. As a verb, as in *bow and curtsy* it rhymes with *bough* (as in tree); as a noun, as in *bow and arrow* it rhymes with *no* not *now*.

C   When you are talking you can check if the other person is understanding you (and he can always interrupt and ask you if he isn't). You usually know how much the other person knows already (so that you don't have to spell it out — it is assumed knowledge). For instance, you both know who *he* is if you start to talk about someone who has just walked past. When you are writing you can't check or assume as much, so you have to be more precise (e.g., in passage 2: *two stewardesses* instead of 'these two girls'). So, writing is normally more precise.

D   When you are talking, the way that you say something (e.g., which words you stress, the look on your face while you're saying it, how loudly you say it, the tone of your voice, etc.) makes clear the meaning. With the same words you can express a whole variety of different meanings — as the next exercise indicates.

Stress and intonation

Say the following in as many different ways as possible in order to give as many different meanings as possible. (Don't change any of the words — just the emphasis and expression you give them.)

1) Good morning.   3) What's your name?

2) Come in. Sit down.   4) I like that.

With writing, these non-verbal features are missing, so that we have to be more precise, and indicate in words, for instance, how the words were said — angrily, gently, sarcastically, jokingly, heartily, seriously, sadly, sympathetically, loudly, softly, etc. So again — writing will need to be more precise and detailed.

E   When you're writing it doesn't matter if you stop for a few minutes to try and work out the most precise way of expressing your meaning. You can afford to be precise. When you're talking to someone, though, a long gap in the conversation can sometimes be embarrassing, so you tend to keep talking — even if it means repeating yourself. Most people do this, even if they have to use colloquial clichés they wouldn't normally use when writing — e.g., from passage A *just fabulous*, *madly in love*, *how far away can you get*, etc. After all, you are having to 'think on your feet' so you can't expect every word to be a literary gem.

When you run out of anything substantial to say you will probably use some sort of 'filler' like *you know*, *I mean*, *'sort of'* — and to smooth the way you will probably have started with *mm*, *er*, *well* or *now*. All this would be quite unnecessary in writing: it is common and understandable (though arguably still not commendable) in speech. So, again, writing has the time to be precise. It does not need to repeat itself or fill out the silence with empty phrases (empty in terms of content, not function — they are, after all, doing the useful job of filling up the silence and keeping the conversation, and thus the relationship, going).

F   When we speak, all sorts of things happen to the sounds we think we are making (associating them, as we tend to, with the written forms). They often change from their written form — which is often accurate if the word is spoken, with emphasis, and on its own, but does not always represent what happens to the word when it is used in connected speech. Thus *connected speech* often leaves out certain sounds or mixes them — for example:

(a) *roas*(t) *beef* *fas*(t) *cars*	} consonant left out
(b) *practiswimming* (practise swimming) *nicetory* (nice story) *baycakes* (bake cakes)	} consonant held — sound slides on
(c) *hafto* (have to) *doeshe* (does she) *wumpiece* (one piece)	} sounds alter
(d) *look at it* *not at all* *a lot of us*	} several words mingle into one sound: liaison of sounds
(e) *beforavowel* (before a vowel) *theyEnglish* (the English) *theyother* (the other) *towanser* (to answer)	} gliding of one sound into another, one word into another may be helped by an extra sound being added which would not exist if the words were spoken separately.

One problem then is that when we speak we don't separate each word as we do when writing. If we did, people would think us rather strange. Instead we run words together, often mixing or altering the sounds (as in the examples above). Sometimes, even if the sound doesn't change, students can still be confused by the words running together in speech. For instance, I have occasionally found students writing *alot* instead of 'a lot' — presumably because that is the way they would *say* the two words. In this connection I was interested to see the following in a report by the Examiners of the AEB O-Level English Language paper for 1978:

There seemed to be an increasing tendency for many candidates to write as one word two separate ones — for example, *along time ago; Ithink; inorder to; aneverending strip* and *alot*.

This kind of mistake is quite understandable. It simply reflects the way people actually speak. *But* it is important to remember that, in writing, every single word should be separate and distinct. In the examples just given what should the separate words have been?

G Another difference is the way we emphasise words in speech as against writing. When speaking we can emphasise a word or phrase by, for instance, stressing it, or by saying it more loudly, or by making a significant pause before it, or by some accompanying gesture (e.g. banging on the table, wagging a finger, etc.) — to make it stand out from the rest of what we are saying.

When writing, we have to use other methods to make the words stand out. We use CAPITAL LETTERS, underlining or exclamation marks!!! In print authors use *italic*, **bold** and even ***bold italic*** letters.

However, writing (except, for instance, personal letters to friends, which can be very near to the way we speak) should normally be a little more 'sober'. So normally you should ration the emphases, and not use too many exclamation or question marks.

Exercise 1.5

Summary

1) *Written and spoken English*
Some of the information you have read so far will probably have been new to you. To check if it has all made sense try this: list all the characteristics of written English in one column, giving an example of each point. Now do the same for spoken English. Do the differences seem clear?

2) Here are a few questions to see how well you can see the differences between written English and spoken English:

    (i) Can you think of seven different ways of spelling the sound *ee*?

    (ii) Can you think of six different sounds the letter *a* might have?

    (iii) George Bernard Shaw used to get very angry about our strange spellings. To show the problems he once wrote the word *fish* as *ghoti*. How do you think he managed it?

The answers are on p. 10.

3) Below you will find four short passages. Some originally appeared in written form, but the rest were originally spoken.

    (i) Decide whether each passage was originally written or spoken.

    (ii) List as many reasons for your decision as possible in each case.

(Are there any aspects which *weren't* covered in my description of speaking as against writing?)

(a) When you leave the house you go back towards the main road until you come to the post office — you remember — we went to the pub opposite last night. Then you see a set of traffic lights straight ahead where the main road crosses the one you're on. Go straight over at the lights and keep on going in that direction for about a mile and a half. It's built up all the way so for goodness sake watch your speed. Then you'll see a big park with green railings on the left — oh, I forgot, they're digging up that bit of road so there's a diversion.

(b) 25 miles: Leave Winsham by A672 forking right at Green Man Hotel. 27 miles: Traffic lights. Turn left onto A67 for 10 miles, passing through Swafield. Hump-backed bridge. Single-line traffic in Town Centre and Greater Millborough. Left for 4½ miles to A6. Caution: Heavy loads entering and leaving Power Station.

(c) You see that bit there. Well if you pull it over this way you'll see the switch. Right? Then press that way and have a look at the pressure here. Once its going fast enough the stuff will come out of that spout thing. There we go. Watch your fingers underneath. There, you see what I mean.

(*d*) After removal the water pump should be dismantled as follows. Remove the bearing locating screws and the countersunk bolt and nut securing the backing plate. Remove the plate and its gasket.

4) Read the following passage. It is the script of a conversation between two women from Liverpool. Then

(i) List the different features which tell you it was originally *Spoken* English. For each feature give an example.

(ii) Translate this passage into acceptable *Written* English.

1st Woman: We don't have no peace at all round, with the vandals round 'ere. I mean every other night you're in bed you can hear 'em on the roofs takin' the lead. One night — ooh a few weeks ago — lady, she's moved now, I heard her screams — they were terrible. I thought maybe she was in a fight or something. I come out — she had her head out of the window crying — no husband — they'd stripped the lead off an' they were still there, with a dog, still there — an' they were actually hanging from that hairdressers over there — with the lead. And — erm — it wasn't for me to say who they were because for the simple reason that if I had o' done it wouldn't ha' been worth living — you know what I mean. I did see some people but it was just the backs o' them. I told her the next morning.

2nd Woman: An' it was that morning that me dad went over to Mick's and these same two boys that got hold of him — up against the wall — an' they said, "You're nosing'," and me dad said, "I'm not. Go play with your toys sonny". He turned round and said, "I'll screw your neck, he said, "if you go and inform on us".

1st Woman: Of course she went at him with th' umbrella.

2nd Woman: Well I mean naturally. He's mi father. He's 79. He's not a young lad. He's done his work. I mean he's not like half of 'em round here standing on the corner. He's gone out to work. He's worked hard for us and I run at him with the umbrella. I said about screwin' his neck I said "I'll screw yourn". I couldn't help it in temper.

Answers to Exercise 1.5, Question 2, p. 9

(i) The sound *ee* is spelt differently, for example, in each of these words: k*e*y, qu*ay*side, gr*ee*n, rec*ei*ve, pl*ea*se, gr*ie*ve, mach*i*ne.

(ii) The letter *a* is pronounced differently, for instance, in each of these words: *a*fter, c*a*ge, *a*ll, *a*bout, f*a*t, vill*a*ge.

(iii) *gh* = *f*, as in *rough*; *o* = *i*, as in *women*; *ti* = *sh*, as in *nation*. Therefore *fish* = *ghoti*!

2 Effective talking

Giving a talk

Giving a talk is not the most common form of verbal communication; it is not as common as just talking to your friends, for instance. However, if you ever become involved in management, trade union activity, teaching, politics, the organisation of a club or society etc., you may find the ability to talk to a group or meeting useful. (It is also, incidentally, one of the easiest forms of verbal communication to mark with some degree of accuracy — hence its inclusion on many courses.)

Preparation: getting used to talking in public

There is a whole variety of exercises available to get you talking as part of a group, and thus build your confidence before giving a solo performance. One simple one is *the snowball story*. The class splits into small groups. Within each group one person starts to tell a story. At a signal he stops and the next person must continue it. This continues until every member of the group has made several contributions and the story is complete.

Details of more complicated exercises are given later, e.g. *Survivors, Murder Most Foul, Jungle Expedition, A Demonstration, A New Deal.*

Giving a talk: some practical hints

Imagine that you have been asked to give a talk, lasting 3–5 minutes, on a topic that interests you:

Before the talk: preparation

A Choose something you are *genuinely* interested in, as this will help you to be more enthusiastic. (And don't say you have no interests — no one can be *that* boring!)

B Jot down, over a period of time, anything that comes to mind. It is better to start with too much than too little — and it gives you confidence to know you have plenty to talk about. (The section on Essays, 'What's your problem?' on p. 112 might help you think of things to say about your subject.)

C   Think of a good start and a good ending — to give your talk a positive approach. An interesting or amusing example or anecdote could be useful here; it's always useful to get the audience on your side.

D   Practise and rehearse your talk: if you are shy, talk to the mirror or your dog; if you have sympathetic friends or relatives, use them as an audience. In particular: (i) check that the talk is the right length; (ii) check that you have a positive start and finish; and (iii) see what works and what doesn't.

E   As you get to know the talk, reduce it to a series of main point headings — only as many as will fit on a postcard.

Practical Point: If you are nervous when standing in front of your group a postcard will not shake as much as a sheet of paper!

I usually give my groups two sample talks for them to comment on — the 'good' one is based on these words on a postcard:

Show one

Professionals

Why?

Chopped heads

Periscope e.g. Telescope effects

Ordinary camera

Just about anything, anywhere, anytime

The talk is on 'Single Lens Reflex Cameras' incidentally, and my positive start (see part C above) is to show the group my camera. My positive end goes something like this —

So, with this sort of camera, and the right lenses, you can take just about any kind of picture, anywhere, and anytime.

It is not a masterpiece of rhetoric, but it does sum up fairly clearly the advantages of the particular type of camera.

F Relaxing methods: (i) more practice = more confidence;

(ii) take two or three big deep breaths;

(iii) relax your neck and shoulders;

(iv) take your time coming out and getting ready;

(v) be sure to look at everyone first — catch their eye — talk to *them*, not to the desk or the ceiling.

Exercise 2.1

Actually giving a talk

Here is the script for the other sample talk I gave on SLR cameras — the 'not so good' one. Read through it and, as you do, (i) make a list of all the mistakes made (as far as giving a talk is concerned) and (ii) by each mistake list what *should* have been done to be more effective. (For the full effect you could ask someone to actually read it as scripted.)

Stage directions. *Read the notes, word for word, while sitting down. As the handwriting is poor, stare at the paper trying to decipher the words. If you look up (at the ceiling not the rest of the class) you will tend to lose your place and take a few seconds to find it again. Speak in a monotone dull drone. As you are nervous the paper shakes.*

(Hesitantly, apologetically) — Er — shall I start — mm — it's not really three minutes — does it have to be? Well — er — I'm going to talk about — er — single lens or reflex cameras — mm — they're called that to distinguish them from twin lens reflex cameras — and the reflex bit — that's to distinguish them from coupled range finder cameras — and Instamatics and things like that — its all done with mirrors and prisms — so you can see better — and put more lenses on — there's lots of lenses available — though it depends what make you get — Russians and East Germans are the cheapest — but they haven't as many lenses — still they've got enough I suppose — well the lenses vary — there's telephoto and mirror lenses — you can hand hold those — and wide angles and fish eyes — oh, and zooms — then there's macro lenses and bellows — and close up lenses er — is it three minutes yet? Well I've got an SLR — that's the abbreviation — it's a Yashica FR — I used to have TL Electros — two of them — but I sold them — they'd only got average metering — the FR's got centre weighted — and it's got LED readouts — I didn't know whether to get that or a Pentax ME — but I wanted to do available light work so I got the FR — with a 1.4 it was still cheaper than the 1.7 Pentax — er . . . *(just happens to stop)*

Exercise 2.2

That of course is how *not* to give a talk. To give a good talk, then, basically do the opposite. There follows a sample marking scheme for a talk (O-level standard): discuss how reasonable it seems. Also, take heart from the fact that anyone who talks for the required time, in a fairly connected way, loudly enough to be heard, and without reading the speech would normally score at least a pass mark.

The following was a mark scheme for a College Mode 3 O-level English Language Oral Examination (where each student was required to give a 3–5 minute talk entitled 'If I were . . .' and then answer questions on it). The marks were out of 10. How fair do you think it was?

7+ (Outstanding)	This is an outstanding oral. The voice is totally clear and audible. There is plenty of appropriate variety of stress and intonation, and appropriate variety of pace and volume to reinforce the content. The manner is confident and relaxed. Preparation has clearly been thorough and has produced excellent timing, a start that catches the attention, a body that sustains it and an ending that draws the whole to an appropriate and definite conclusion (e.g. twist/new angle/concise summary/neat rounding off). The quality of content and ideas is high and the viewpoint e.g. novel/authoritative. Level of involvement clearly high. Clear, logical, coherent progression of ideas — transparently so. Questions not only understood but answered at same high level as rest of talk. Varied and appropriate vocabulary, sentence structure etc.
6 (Good)	This is clearly a good talk — going beyond normal standards in most of the following areas: content, preparation, clarity, coherence, interest, voice, manner, understanding, responsiveness etc., and perhaps being outstanding in certain areas, but lacking that sustained, complete and overall excellence of 7+ above. Perhaps a mark for the articulate enthusiast who lacks a few of the more rhetorical techniques of 7+ above, but is clearly well above average standard.
5 (Reasonable: a pass)	The student speaks reasonably clearly and audibly, and his voice communicates and sustains interest. There is evidence of reasonable preparation (e.g. good timing, an attempt to start in an interesting manner and make a definite conclusion etc.). The talk will proceed in a reasonably coherent and logical manner. The content of the talk will be of some interest and include e.g. interesting/useful/unusual ideas. A sustained account. The student will be able to understand and respond to any follow-up questions. A somewhat limited command of/ variety of English might confine what would otherwise be a good account to this level.

4 (Attempt that doesn't quite succeed)	The student *attempts* to produce the points indicated above (5+), e.g. interesting voice/manner/content, adequate preparation and understanding, coherent progression, but does not quite succeed due to failures in *some* (but by no means all) of the above. Not a fully *sustained* account. Perhaps for the talk that starts well but then runs out of steam, indicating imperfect preparation.
3 (Very limited performance)	The student makes some, limited attempt — but has clearly not understood or realised what is required and fails to reach the required standard in *most* areas (e.g. voice/manner/content/preparation/coherence/understanding etc.). May also be given to a student who simply reads from notes and makes no attempt to 'give a talk'.
2 (Totally inadequate. The mark is for at least turning up and making an attempt)	The student has obviously made practically no attempt to prepare (e.g. timing way out, no clear beginning or end). His ideas are boring and clichéd and no attempt has been made to think them through. Manner and voice — monotonous/soporific/panic-stricken. No coherence or logic of sequence. Questions not understood and/or inappropriate response.
0	The student is absent without a genuine and provable (e.g. letter from home indicating reason) excuse. He should not be given a second chance to do the oral. Automatic zero mark.

One important point that is perhaps missing from the mark scheme is **Awareness of context** — by which I mean, for instance:

● Are you giving your talk to 5 people or to 50?

● Will you be speaking in a large room or a small one, and will it be empty or full?

● Who is your audience? Are they young or old, male or female, experts or laymen? Do they know you?

● Why are you giving a talk? Are you trying to persuade people about something, to entertain them, to give them information etc.?

● Is your audience friendly, or perhaps not so friendly?

The more aware you are of these factors the more you can aim to adjust your talk accordingly. This might affect how loudly you speak, whether you use simple or complicated language, whether you try to be serious or amusing, what kind of examples you use etc.

So, in the exercises that follow, remember to ask:

15

- *Who* am I talking to?
- *Where* am I giving the talk, and
- *Why*?

This will help you decide *what* to say and *how* to say it!

Exercise 2.3

1) This question was triggered off by the essay question:

What factors do you think ought to govern the amount of money people are paid for the work they do?

Choose one of the occupations from the list below. You now have 20 minutes to prepare a pay claim, stating why your particular choice deserves a pay rise more than any of the others. Then put your case to the rest of the class. They should then vote on how convincingly your case was argued (rather than on what their own feelings were previously).

(How fair is it to label the respective occupations 'male' and 'female' incidentally?)

Male	Female
Miner	Housewife
Bank Manager	Nurse
Dustman	Doctor
Clerk	Cleaner
Managing Director of ICI	Secretary/Typist
Window Cleaner	Factory Worker
Salesman	Masseuse
Newsagent	Shop Assistant
Advertising Artist	Hairdresser
Pop Singer	Social Worker
Professional Footballer	Primary School Teacher
Car Worker	Film Star

2) Prepare a three-minute talk on *one* of the following:
   (i) A demonstration of some skill or process.
   (ii) A hobby or interest.
   (iii) 'If I were . . .'

3) After requests from students your school/college has just set up its own internal radio station, run by the students, and operating, for an experimental period of one term, from 12 to 2 each day. You have been given the job of preparing a two-minute news broadcast to be given at 1 o'clock each day.

Prepare the script for such a broadcast for each of three successive days, using the morning newspapers to prepare a brief summary of the major items. As the programming schedule is very tight you must ensure that each news broadcast does last for just 2 minutes. (This will be timed.)

4) Choose one area or aspect of the school/college you consider to be in need of change and improvement. It will be your job to persuade a meeting of the School Council/Student Union (simulated by the class itself, or several classes combined) that change and improvement are needed, by means of a short speech lasting 3–5 minutes. (Different members of the class should take it in turns to chair the meeting, and to act as secretary, producing minutes of the meeting — which could also be taped or videoed, should facilities be available.)

5) Prepare a talk, 'An Introduction to . . .' (the course you are following at the moment). The talk should be of roughly five minutes' length and suitable for inclusion in a radio programme for schools and colleges entitled 'Courses at 16+: The Alternatives'. Each talk will be taped — and the best talks will be played to new and prospective students next year.

Write a *script* for the talk (with directions, as necessary, on how it should be given). Before the script, write an Introduction which indicates how your talk has taken into account:

(i)   the intended audience;

(ii) the medium used (radio/cassette);

(iii) the suitability of the topic in terms of (i) and (ii) above.

Interviews

Before you are offered a job, or a place at a college, polytechnic or university you will usually have to attend an interview. To help you perform as well as possible here are several check lists:

Getting the interview

- Did you make a photocopy of the application form and fill that in first — asking a friend, parent or teacher to check that what you had written was *neat*, *accurate* and answered *all* the questions?

- Did you then fill in the *original* application form from the corrected photocopy, thus making sure the form you sent off had no mistakes, and leaving you the photocopy for future use?

- Did you give as referees people who have known you for some time, who hold responsible positions, and who would be likely to say complimentary things about you?

Before the interview

- Have you collected together all the relevant documents to take with you (any letters or information already sent to you; the photocopy of your application form; anything you have specifically been asked to take — a passport-sized photograph, examination certificates, testimonials, a medical certificate etc.)?

- Do you know *exactly* where the interview is, and how to get there?

- Have you arranged to get there in plenty of time — checking bus or train timetables, arranging a lift etc.?

- Are you dressed smartly, and looking neat and tidy — so that you will give a good first impression?

- Have you thought about what sort of questions you're likely to be asked, and what sort of answers to give? (If not, have a look at the list of common interview questions later in this section.)

- Have you any idea *what sort of person* the interviewer is likely to be looking for — someone keen/reliable/confident/hardworking/quiet/neat and tidy/sociable/lively/intelligent/attractive or whatever other qualities are considered important? Are you that sort of person?

  The qualities will vary, of course. The sort of qualities that make a good bunny girl, for instance, may not seem so important when choosing an engineering graduate or a plumber!

- If you are shown round the firm, college etc., before the full interview, do you realise that the people who show you round may also be asked for their opinions of you? So look interested, and use this opportunity to ask useful questions, such as: is this a good firm to work for? what are the prospects of promotion? what about possible redundancy? what facilities are there? etc.

During the interview

To help give a good impression, do you:
- look interested?
- speak clearly and sensibly?
- sit reasonably still and straight (rather than slouching, fidgeting etc.)?
- look at whoever is talking to you, or asking you questions (if there are several people at the interview)?

The application form will already have shown the basic facts about you — how old you are, what qualifications you have, what your work experience is etc. And the interviewer may well go through these points either to confirm them or to put you at your ease. However, what the interview is really for is to find out *what sort of person you are* — something your application form can only hint at. You will therefore be judged, partly by your appearance, partly by your answers, and partly by your manner. What the interviewers will be trying to find out are things like:

- Do you really want the job?
- Do you know what it involves?
- Will you be good at your work?
- Will you get on with other people — bosses, customers, workmates, colleagues?
- Is your character right for the job?

When you look at the list of common interview questions which follows, try to decide what sort of thing the interviewer is really trying to find out about you.

Common questions at job interviews

- How long have you had this sort of job in mind?
- Why do you want to do this particular job?
- Why do you want to work for this particular firm?
- What previous work experience have you had?
- What were the people you worked with like? Did you get on with them?
- Which school did you go to? Did you enjoy it? Why/Why not?
- Did you hold any positions of responsibility while at school?
- What were your favourite subjects?
- What sort of course are you doing at the moment?
- Tell me something about your hobbies or interests — what do you enjoy doing most?
- Is there much social life where you live?
- What do you do in your spare time?
- Can you type? Do you drive?
- What kind of work would you like to do to begin with?
- Are you applying for many other jobs at the moment?
- How well would you say you got on with other people?
- Would you be prepared to study while working with us — in order to get further qualifications?
- What would your attitude be to working overtime/weekends/short time?
- Would you mind being transferred to another area?

- How easy will it be for you to travel to work?
- What do you see yourself doing in another five years' time?
- Is there anything you would like to ask me?

Exercise 2.4

1) **Common questions at college/polytechnic/university interviews**

From what you have read so far try to work out 20 possible questions you might be asked at an interview to gain a place in Further or Higher Education. Remember that the emphasis in this kind of interview will be rather different, and will be on your educational ability in particular.

2) Reply to this advertisement:

POST CLASSIFIED

FREE SERVICE

To Unemployed Youngsters

From August 6th a special classification entitled 'Jobs Wanted — School Leavers' will be appearing daily in the Evening Post.

If you are under 18 and still seeking a job you are invited to submit your advertisement and it will be published free of charge.

Tell prospective employers about yourself, about your education and about the kind of job you are looking for. Keep your advertisement to within 50 words and include your full name and address and also your telephone number if you have one.

Send it, marking the envelope 'School Leavers Column' to:-

Ann Menzies Neal,
Classified Sales Manager,
Yorkshire Post Newspapers Ltd.,
Wellington Street,
Leeds LS1.

P.S. If you get a job from your advertisement, Ann will be delighted to hear the good news.

3) First, check that you know what the following are:

(*a*) A Personnel Manager

(*b*) Mobility

(*c*) References

(*d*) A job description

(*e*) A testimonial

(*f*) A short list

Then:

(i) Collect as much material as you can on a type of job you are interested in (for instance, using material from the Careers section of your school/college/library; for instance, talking to people who know about that sort of job).

(ii) From this material prepare a job description, of the kind a Personnel Manager might draw up when trying to decide what sort of person to appoint, and of the kind that could be sent to applicants to explain what the job would involve.

(iii) From this material also prepare a job advertisement, of the kind that might appear in the 'Situations Vacant' section of a newspaper.

(iv) Prepare also an application form, suitable for this kind of job, designed to give the kind of information needed to check if applicants measure up to the job description.

(v) Then, fill in the application form to the best of your ability, including giving referees.

(vi) Staple together the job description, job advertisement and completed application forms, and circulate them round the class for discussion, suggested improvements, evaluation, etc.

(vii) Those students who are agreed to have completed their application forms effectively will be interviewed for the posts in question.

Group discussion

Earlier we looked at one type of oral communication — giving a talk. More common, however, in everyday life, are occasions when we talk to another person, or to others in small groups (e.g. friends, colleagues, shop assistants, relatives etc.), and when they reply, so that there is *dialogue*. A similar, if perhaps more formal type of communication occurs in meetings (e.g. committee meetings).

Different people communicate in different ways in groups. Shortly we shall look at different suggestions — based on observations of people actually communicating in groups.

Perhaps the most useful lesson *you*, as a student, can learn from these suggestions is *how many different ways* it is possible to communicate. When you do the exercises that follow try dividing the class in half. One half will act as the group and discuss the exercise. The other half will observe the technique they use. (It is easier for each observer to watch and make notes on a different student — and then report back after the discussion.)

One thing many students find at first is that, although they feel they are using a variety of techniques, most of what the observers find they are doing is proposing, supporting, defending or attacking. Some techniques such as 'open behaviour' (e.g. admitting mistakes) or bringing other people into the discussion and asking their opinions are very rarely used. It is also noted that some students may try to get involved in the discussion, but each time they start to speak, a more vocal student will start to speak as well, not giving them a chance. Again, some students will try to dominate the discussion, and perhaps cause resentment among the others. As the exercises continue, and as the students find out more about the ways in which groups operate, however, some students may try new techniques. Often they will find that this wider range helps them to be more successful, and helps the group work more smoothly or efficiently. Try doing this yourself.

Group discussion, group behaviour

To help you use a variety of techniques when discussing, and to describe what other people do in discussions, here are some suggested definitions. You might not agree with every definition, or you might feel some techniques have been missed out. If so, amend the list for your own use. This is just to start you thinking . . .

Proposing. Putting forward a new idea, suggestion or proposal — e.g. 'Why don't we . . . ?'

Building. Taking a proposal suggested by someone else, and developing it, or adding to it — e.g. 'Yes, and then we could . . .'

Supporting. Agreeing with someone else's idea — and explaining *why* you agree — e.g. 'That seems sensible. It would solve the problem of . . .'

Disagreeing. Disagreeing with someone else's idea — but explaining *why* you disagree — e.g. 'I'm not sure. Aren't you forgetting about . . . ?'

Defending. Agreeing with someone, but giving no good reason — e.g. 'I agree!'

Attacking.	Disagreeing with someone, but giving no good reason — e.g. 'Well, I don't (agree) . . .'
Blocking.	Trying to block a suggestion, but giving no good reason, and suggesting no alternative — e.g. 'It won't work,' 'We can't do that.'*
Open.	Willing to admit a mistake or lack of ability in some areas — e.g. 'Yes, perhaps I was wrong to . . .'. 'Yes, looking back I didn't handle that too well, did I?'†
Testing understanding.	Checking an earlier point has been understood — e.g. 'Are we all clear about what Janet was saying? If we . . . then we must also . . .'.
Summarising.	Summarising what has been said so far (i.e. the main points of the discussion, or a part of the discussion, restated briefly — e.g. 'So we're all agreed then. We've decided to . . . and . . .'.
Seeking information.	Finding out information (facts, figures, opinions etc.) — e.g. 'So how much will this cost altogether?' 'What do you two think?'
Giving information.	Offering information (facts, figures, opinions etc.) — e.g. 'John couldn't make it today. But he asked me to tell you . . .'.

*Bald statements like the above are blocking statements, but if the speaker had said, 'It won't work. If we . . . then . . . and in any case . . .,' he would have been giving reasons and thus disagreeing rather than just blocking. Also, defending and attacking behaviour are used towards another *person*; blocking is against an *idea* or *suggestion*.

†As people are often unwilling to admit their own mistakes or failings this technique is sometimes not used. However, it can be very useful. If you are under attack, stubborn resistance to criticism may lead to more criticism — while simply admitting a mistake (perhaps with an 'extenuating' circumstance) can cut the ground away beneath your critic's feet. If someone continues to criticise you even after you have admitted a mistake, you will normally pick up sympathy from others who will then feel your opponent is taking things too far.

Paradoxically, open behaviour is often used by confident and successful people. They are sufficiently confident of their general ability to be willing to admit to a few mistakes, and astute enough to realise its effectiveness in meeting justified criticism. People who insist that they are always right aren't always too popular. Making the odd mistake, and admitting it, simply shows you are human too.

Exercise 2.5

Here's an opportunity to try out the techniques mentioned. It will probably work best if half of you act as the committee, and the other half as observers, making notes on the techniques used, and then reporting back on what you saw and heard.

Survivors

It is the year after World War Three and most of the world's population is dead. The survivors live in nuclear shelters underground, where they must remain until it is safe to return to the surface. You are members of a committee set up to decide how the survivors should be trained or retrained to be of maximum usefulness (a) during the long period underground, and (b) when they return to the surface. As a committee you must decide on, and make a list of, the order of importance of the following occupations as far as training priorities are concerned:

Nurse	Farmer
Telecommunications engineer	Soldier
Dentist	Carpenter
Musician	Blacksmith
Teacher	Waste disposal expert
Tailor	Fisherman
Actor	Doctor
Miner	

Group discussion: problems of observing

If you were observing, did you find it difficult to listen to the discussion, *and* watch it, *and* think what different techniques were being used, *and* make notes on them? If so, don't worry — people usually find it difficult the first few times.

To make it easier:

(i) Just watch *one* person and note what he or she does.

(ii) Once you've watched a few discussions, you'll be clearer in your mind what techniques are being used.

(iii) Prepare a checklist *before* the discussion, and just write a stroke each time a particular technique is used. These can be added up once the discussion is over.

e.g. *Observation on student A during a discussion*

Proposing	⊬⊬⊤ ‖	7 times	*Supporting*	⊬⊬⊤ ⊬⊬⊤	10 times
Building	‖	2 times	*Disagreeing*	‖‖	3 times
etc.					

(iv) If possible, tape (or even videotape) the discussion. That way you can play it back as often as you need to for discussion of the techniques used.

24

(v) As there are so many techniques, and perhaps some behaviour that wasn't covered in my earlier suggestions (e.g. not just *what* people said, but also *why*; were they trying to help the group reach a decision?; were they trying to give a good impression of themselves etc?) have a look at this slightly different way of analysing group behaviour. It is particularly useful because it groups the behaviour under three main headings, which makes it easier to handle:

Task-centred/Relationship-centred/Self-centred

Task-centred	Proposing
	Information-seeking
	Information-giving
	Clarifying/testing understanding
	Evaluating/summarising
	Dissenting
Relationship-centred	Active listening (seeming interested in what other people say)
	Refereeing (if disputes arise)
	Bringing in (the quieter members of the group)
	Reducing tension
	Compromising
	Seeking feelings
Self-centred	Blocking
	Defending/attacking
	Shutting out (not letting other people get a word in)
	Dominating
	Avoiding
	Seeking recognition
	Nit-picking

Where the members of the group are most concerned to achieve an objective (e.g to reach the best decision in a limited time) they will probably use 'task-centred' techniques.

If the group meets regularly, and its members are friends, rather than offend other members of the group they will probably tend to use 'relationship-centred' techniques — even if this means postponing or avoiding a controversial decision.

Where the members of the group are most concerned about themselves and their own 'images', the objective and the other members of the group may tend to be used simply as means to that end.

25

Now try the following. If possible half of you should act as the jury and half as observers, changing places after each case.

Exercise 2.6

Discussion: murder most foul?

Below are details of some murder cases. In each case your group should try to operate as a jury, i.e. discuss the case, and try to reach a *unanimous decision* on whether the accused was guilty of murder (Some of the cases may seem rather old, but they are not out of date and occur in many modern law books because they raise interesting questions about murder.)

To help you decide here are some basic principles of law. Normally to be guilty of a crime the accused must have

- performed a *guilty action* (i.e. a criminal act)
- with a guilty *intent* (i.e. it was not an accident, or even negligent — but done deliberately).

The guilty intent need not be to do *exactly* what actually happens but must be something very similar. For instance, if you hit someone hard on the head repeatedly with a sledgehammer, with intent to commit grievous bodily harm, and they die, that should have been a result you might reasonably have expected and you would be guilty of murder. However, if you push someone aside, feeling annoyed with them, and they die of a heart attack, that would be such an unexpected consequence that you would not be guilty of murder because you would have had no intent to commit murder or grievous bodily harm.

(a) **R. v. Hyam (1974)**

Hyam was the lover of Jones. She became suspicious of his relationship with another woman. When she heard that he was intending to go on holiday with the woman Hyam went to her house. She poured petrol through the letter box and then pushed newspaper in. She lit the paper and caused a fierce fire. She left without raising the alarm. Two girls who were in the house with their mother were killed. Hyam said that she merely intended to frighten the woman. There was evidence that before setting the fire she had checked that Jones was at his own home so that he did not come to any harm.

(b) **R. v. Saunders & Archer (1573)**

John Saunders had a wife whom he intended to kill, in order that he might marry another woman with whom he was in love ... the said John Saunders ... gave (poison) to her, being sick, in a roasted apple, and she eat a small part of it, and gave the rest to ... Eleanor Saunders, an infant, about three years of age, who was the daughter of her and the said John Saunders ... (who) seeing it blamed his wife for it, and said that apples were not good for such infants; to which his wife replied that they were better for such infants than for herself: and the daughter eat the poisoned apple, and the said John Saunders, her father, saw her eat it, and did not offer to take it from her lest he should be suspected, and afterwards the wife recovered, and his daughter died of the said poison.

Whether or no this was murder . . . was somewhat doubted, for he had no intent to poison his daughter . . . and he did not give her the poison, but his wife ignorantly gave it her.

(c)   **R. v. Smith (1959) (on appeal)**

The appellant, a soldier, was charged with, and convicted of, the murder of a soldier during the course of a fight between the men of two regiments who shared the same barrack room. The deceased received two bayonet wounds, one in the arm, and one in the back which pierced the lung and caused haemorrhage. Another soldier tried to carry the wounded man to the medical reception station. He twice dropped him to the ground. At the station the medical officer and his orderly were extremely busy. There were two other stabbed men to deal with as well as others with minor injuries. The medical staff did not know of the haemorrhage nor was the serious nature of the injury realised. A transfusion of saline solution was tried but failed, and when breathing seemed impaired oxygen and artificial respiration were given. This treatment was 'thoroughly bad' and might well have affected his chance of recovery. There was medical evidence at the trial that haemorrhage of this type tends to stop. Had there been a blood transfusion available chances of recovery were assessed as high as 75 per cent by a medical witness for the defence.

(These three cases are from *A Casebook on Criminal Law* by
D W Elliott and J C Wood)

(d)   **R. v. Blaue (1975)**

The accused stabbed a girl. She was taken to hospital, where according to doctors a blood transfusion would probably have saved her life. However, she was a Jehovah's Witness, refused a blood transfusion, and died.

Group discussion: quantity versus quality

So far we've been looking more at quantity than quality — for instance, at *how many* techniques a person used, and *how often*. This is useful if we are trying to encourage people to use new discussion techniques. It is also easy to keep a record of.

However, the person who uses the greatest variety of techniques isn't necessarily the most effective member of the group — just as the person who talks most isn't necessarily the most effective. It's not *how much* you say, so much as *what you say and how* you say it.

Knowing effective discussion techniques is useful – but knowing *when* to use them is also important.

How can you check who is being most effective in a discussion? Here are a few suggestions:

A   Don't just count the number of proposals a person makes. Check how many of them are actually followed up by the rest of the group.

B   How easy does each person find it to get a hearing? Do others automatically stop to listen – or does he have difficulty getting a word in? Do others show approval of what he is saying (by nodding, making sounds of agreement, listening more intently etc.) – or do they show a lack of interest (whispering to friends, looking bored etc.) or a lack of agreement (butting in to object, shaking their heads, frowning etc.)?

C   Do others take his word – or do they question or doubt what he says?

D   What part does he play (i) in keeping the group together, (ii) in keeping to the task in hand (being a good listener, asking other people's opinions, avoiding disputes, and generally keeping the discussion moving if it looks like getting sidetracked etc.)?

In the exercise that follows look for the *quality* of contributions in particular:

Exercise 2.7

Jungle expedition

1)   *Individual work* – do this part without talking to anyone else!

You have just gained a job as a driver with an archaeological expedition, exploring an ancient ruined city deep in the jungles of South America – ten days' drive by Land Rover from the nearest village, following rough jungle tracks. It will be your job to ferry new archaeological equipment and supplies to the city. Half way along your very first journey, bringing equipment and a new member to join the expedition, you find the track flooded and take an alternative route. Several hours later you realise you are lost. You try to find your way back but the Land Rover becomes stuck in swampy ground and slowly starts to sink in the mud. If the Land Rover sinks much more, you will be stranded, without supplies, in the middle of a vast uninhabited jungle area. You will not be missed for at least five or six days, and organising a search operation will take some time, with perhaps another five or six days before you are located – if at all! Which of the following items would you take from the Land Rover (in whole or part) to help you survive? List them in order of importance: 1 for the most important, 2 for the next important, and so on up to 18 for the least important:

- a 12 foot length of nylon rope
- 6 mess tins
- 10 packets of salt tablets

- $4 \times 4\frac{1}{2}$ gallon cans of petrol
- 2 maps of the area
  (not necessarily 100 % accurate, as produced by aerial survey only)
- 2 rucksacks
- a medical kit
- 4 large cases of composite rations (mainly in tins)
- 2 Calor Gas stoves
- 3 machetes
- 1 flare pistol
- snakebite serum
- 2 compasses
- 2 spades
- $6 \times 4\frac{1}{2}$ gallon cans of water
- 1 hunting rifle
- mosquito netting
- insect-repellant cream

2) *Group work* — do this as usual, i.e. half the group discussing, the other half observing.

3) Now try to reach a unanimous decision on the *ten* most important items (a Top Ten) and their order of importance.

Some final discussion exercises

1) Knowing that many students in the school/college have, or would like, part-time or holiday jobs, a group of you have decided to set up a Temporary Jobs Information Service, covering jobs in the school's/college's catchment area.

In groups of four or five work out how best:
- (i)   to set up, and
- (ii) to organise, and
- (iii) to run this information service

and then report back to the other groups.

Include a realistic estimate of all resources (including people and time) required.

After this each group should consider how it operated as a group during the above.

Each student should then write a review of his group's activity, i.e.
- (i)   proposals for the Information Service produced by his group
- (ii) how his group functioned as a group
- (iii) his own role within the group.

2) The school/college has been asked to send a small team of staff and students to a local 11–16 secondary school to talk about courses available for 16 + students.

In small groups (three or four people each) work out a short (ten-minute) *illustrated* talk on:

> Life as a sixth-former/further education student/sixth-form college student

which you feel would appeal to the students at the school (without sacrificing accuracy).

Now adapt the talk for a parents' evening at the school.

What, if anything, would you add, leave out, change or amend — and why?

Exercise 2.9

Written exercise on group discussion

To see what you have learnt from all this experience of group discussion write a paragraph on each of the following. Use the paragraphs as a basis for an overall discussion on group work afterwards.

1) The advantages of working as part of a group.

2) Problems that may arise.

3) Ways of overcoming them and improving group discussion.

4) How I behave as a part of a discussion group.

5) Any changes I have noticed in myself or other people while doing work on group communications.

6) Opportunities for group discussion outside of school and college.

7) Possible uses of group discussion techniques in school and college — for instance, to help learning.

3 Would you be so kind?

Varieties of tone and register

Levels of formality

We can all see the difference between formal and informal language, between for instance:

Bring it back if anything goes wrong.

and

Should this product or any part of it become defective under normal use within 12 months of the date of purchase, the defect will be rectified and any defective component parts repaired or replaced.

Partly this is a difference of words.

Exercise 3.1

Sort out the words in the list below into pairs with similar meaning. Then put them into columns marked informal and formal:

terminate	*think*	*function*
tell	*bona fide*	*at first*
initiate	*home*	*require*
genuine	*initially*	*end*
inform	*residence*	*completed*
enough	*start*	*want*
consider	*work*	*finished*
sufficient		

Here is an example:

Informal	Formal
end	*terminate*

Partly it is a difference of precision. Informal language tends to be used between people who know each other and who can therefore

31

take a lot for granted. Formal language is more often used in forms and documents where the exact meaning of the words needs to be clear — even if this means more words and longer words. It's a bit like the difference between talking and writing seen in Chapter 1 — each has its uses.

However, language isn't just formal or informal — it's all sorts of shades between. Asking someone to open a window, for instance, could be done at various levels:

Fairly formal Could you possibly open the window, please
Would you mind opening the window

Semi-formal Could you open the window, please
Open the window please

Fairly informal Open the window
Open it, luv

without even considering more formal flights of fancy, such as:

The opening of the said aperture for the purposes of ventilation, if performed by your esteemed self, would be a source of considerable pleasure to myself and ensure my deepest gratitude.

1) Try this yourself. Find as many ways as possible to express the following, and indicate what level of formality each example is:

   (i) Asking someone to be quiet.

   (ii) Asking someone to marry you.

   (iii) Complimenting someone on what he/she is wearing.

   (iv) Criticising a recently released record.

Copy the table below and fill in the gaps (where possible), and then continue the table by adding a further *five* examples of your own.

Rather formal (posh)	Standard English (semi-formal)	Colloquial (fairly informal)	Slang (very informal)
intoxicated	drunk	tipsy	pissed
gentleman	man	fellow, chap	guy, bloke
	doctor		
police constable			
			kicked the bucket
		cash	
	employer		
	insane		
incarcerated			

Now, briefly explain *when* and *why* it would be appropriate (if at all) to use each of the varieties of English indicated above.

Make a list of the different kinds you have used: (i) so far today, and (ii) during the last week.

Which levels to use when — and why

Rich young man (to beautiful girl drinking Campari at sun-soaked resort):
Were you truly wafted here from Paradise?

Girl: No. Luton Airport.

These days there isn't much of a case for very formal English. It's true that business documents need to be carefully worded. Claims can be made under them or against them amounting to thousands or even millions of pounds, so they need to be able to stand up to close legal investigation of every word. Formal English tends to be more precise than informal so is often used in documents. Even so, semi-formal or standard English is usually enough. Quite simply it is easier for most people to understand. Over-formal English, on the other hand, can lead to cases like this:

A visitor to a government building in Washington DC found a door with this imposing sign:

> **4156**
> **General Services Administration**
> **Region 3**
> **Public Buildings Service**
> **Building Management Division**
> **Utility Room**
> **Custodial**

On asking what it was, he discovered it was a broom cupboard.

Over-formal language, in the shape of official forms, also confuses thousands of ordinary people each year. For example, a question on a form issued by a Yorkshire local authority to its council house tenants asked for 'length of tenancy'. One resident replied, 'Approx. 38 feet'. To meet this problem a group of people have set up a 'form factory' just to simplify official forms and make them more readable. Now try this yourself.

Exercise 3.4

1) Take the following extracts and rewrite them in a less formal style — as if you were writing them for a friend:

(a) Possession of such a letter is not obligatory but should greatly facilitate entry.

(b) Small dogs may, at the discretion of the conductor and at the owner's risk, be carried without charge upon the upper deck of double-decker buses or in single-deck buses. The decision of the conductor is final.

2) Now collect five different examples of 'official English', e.g. notices in the school/college, on public transport, official forms, regulations etc. Then produce more informal versions of the five you have found. Then discuss whether the versions you have produced are better than the originals.

If over-formal English can cause problems, so too can informal English. Sometimes informal English can be *too* personal, as we might find if we tried replacing

NO ENTRY

signs by ones reading

YOU CAN'T COME IN.

It can also be too casual, and thus either offend, mislead or cause extra work for the reader. For instance, writing to a friend you could say, 'about that money you lent me' and (unless you are in the habit of borrowing money from your friend — in which case he might not be a friend much longer) your friend will understand what you are referring to. Writing to a bank, however, where you are just one of many customers, and where many loans are made, you would probably need to be more specific — for instance, 'Last August I borrowed £1000 (to buy a new motor bike).' Remember that one of the advantages of more formal language is that it is often more precise.

Exercise 3.5

To show some of the *dangers* of casual or informal language read the following and then explain how each could be understood in two ways:

(a) You will be lucky to get this student in your class.

(b) If I said you had a beautiful body, would you hold it against me?

(c) Well Margaret, if you've nothing on, why don't I come over?

(d) (To a class of students) I don't think you lot were all there yesterday.

(e) We shall waste no time in dealing with your complaint.

For everyday business purposes, then, a *semi-formal tone* is probably best. It avoids the confusions caused by both overformal and over-casual language and is more universally clear and understandable.

To remind you of the shades of formality, however, and that each has its place, try this exercise:

Exercise 3.6

Consider Michael Trent, aged 40, a Personnel manager, married with 3 children.

In the course of a normal week-day how many different ways might he be addressed — both in speech and writing?

(For example, would his wife address him in the same way as a shop assistant at the newsagent's he calls in at on his way to work?)

Now do the same for:

Christine Ellis, aged 32, a Primary School Teacher, married with one child.

(You should be able to think of at least eight different forms of address for each.)

Exercise 3.7

Now consider the extracts in RSVP below. In particular consider:

1) how you would feel receiving each of these messages,

2) how far the level of formality would be responsible, and

3) whether the level of formality was appropriate.

Exercise 3.8

RSVP

The following extracts from messages all have something in common. In one way or another they all 'request the pleasure' of someone's company — some more forcibly than others. Who is doing the requesting in each case, and how forcibly/persuasively?

In what ways do these messages differ? Consider especially the different varieties of English involved.

(a)

INFORMATION has this day been laid before me,
the undersigned Clerk to the Justices,
by EDWARD PETER BAINES, Chief Constable of the
Newtown Police, for that you,
at Newtown
on the   2nd   day of   November 1980
did drive a motor vehicle, namely, a motor car
on a restricted road called Waterloo Road
at a speed exceeding thirty miles per hour,
contrary to Road Traffic Regulation Act, 1967, section 71, 74, 78
YOU ARE THEREFORE HEREBY SUMMONED to appear
before the MAGISTRATES' COURT, sitting at The Law Courts
                    Simon Road
                    Newtown
on the   15th   day of   April 1981   at the hour of
10.00 a.m. in the forenoon, to answer to the said Information.

(b)

Thanks for the card. Try a winter break in Burnett, if Doncaster dulls the senses. Glad to see you any time.

(c)

Dear Mr
Thank you for your application for the post of   . The
Selection Panel would be very pleased if you could join the
short list of candidates who are being invited to come here
for an interview. In order to be briefed before meeting the
panel, you are asked to report to   at   on
            at   and I should be grateful if you would
telephone my secretary at the above number to say whether
or not you can attend.
The interviews for this post are timed for
                                              in

(d)

CHANCE ENCOUNTER
Soft glow kindles
Sparks of fire leap
Your body next to mine
Tender touch
Taut desire
Alike, unlike, attract, embrace
Mystery and fascination of a chance encounter
Weave spells
For you
For me
For us?

(e)

Lady young, Lady fair
Answer this fond lover's prayer
Box B501

Tone and register

Exercise 3.9

There follows a variety of extracts. Read each one and then answer
the following questions about each.

1) Is this intended to be read or listened to?

2) What kind of person is speaking/writing?

3) What reader/listener has he in mind?

4) What purpose has he in mind?

5) Is the person writing/speaking a man or a woman?

6) Is this modern English, and if not, of what period?

7) Is this 'standard English' (BBC English), and if not, what variety is it?

8) Considering the 'levels of formality' mentioned earlier in this section how would you rate this extract?

9) How serious is such an extract and how can you tell?

10) How appropriate is the language in this extract?

(For all the above try to point to particular words, phrases, or features which illustrate your answer.)

(*a*) Beautiful, breathtaking, bountiful and blessed; mere superlatives inadequate to express all that this tropical island is and has to offer. For the next few days you can believe in Paradise. Nothing is ordinary, everything extraordinarily breathtaking and appealing; the lushness of trees and flowers which make the island one of the greenest in the world, the almost permanent holiday atmosphere engendered by the numerous festivals, and the exotic island feasts under the brilliant stars.

(*b*) N8 F to shr hse, own rm £22 pw 348 5458 evening

NW2 F sh dble bdsit £15 pw 278 6162, ext 100 (9–5)

NW2 Prof f non smoker, o/r £26 pw 450 9143

O/R CH. Col TV. £44 pm. Pref F. Tottenham, after 6.30 pm 740 2662

NW6. 2 gl sh rm. 451 3392

RICHMOND. Twin rm lux hse. £46 pw. tel 948 1104 eve.

(*c*) Jack and Jill went up the hill
To fetch a pail of water
Jack fell down and broke his crown
And Jill came tumbling after.

(*d*) Admit no other way to save his life —
As I subscribe not that, nor any other,
But in the loss of question — that you, his sister,
Finding yourself desired of such a person
Whose credit with the judge, or own great place,
Could fetch your brother from the manacles
Of the all-binding law; and that there were
No earthly mean to save him, but that either
You must lay down the treasures of your body
To this supposed, or else to let him suffer:
What would you do?

(*e*) Get the right hand under butt of rifle, and swing over to the left and bash his head in and if that doesn't work, swing into the right parry. Now the right parry is getting the rifle at the point of balance in the left hand — get the right hand on the butt of the rifle and swing into his balls. Ruin his chances, and then on, 'cos there's plenty more where he just came from.

(f)   Fry at 375°F and test with a frying thermometer; do not heat above 375°F.

Do not fill any frying pan more than ⅓ full and never leave it unattended while frying.

Do not use a lid on your deep frying pan while heating or cooking.

Do not pour hot oil back into the bottle — allow it to cool first.

(g)   I have read a lot of his books and I believe in the existentia..sm very much; although I must admit that I have never been able to finish one of his main books: *La nausée* (in French, I don't know the title in English), I started to read this book a year ago and it made me feel so depressed that I gave up reading it. So, if you ever feel miserable, don't read *La nausée* — a friend's advice.

(h)   The teenage blonde at the centre of the sex-trap murder case is to flee to Italy and a new future after death threats at her Oldham home.

Nineteen-year-old Lauro Andronik, given probation yesterday for the manslaughter of brutal teddy boy John Monk, was today in hiding at a secret address in fear of her life.

(i)   It is the only time that I am thankful for being a woman, that time of evening, when I draw the curtains, take off my old clothes and prepare to go out. Minute by minute the excitement grows. I brush my hair under the light and the colours are autumn leaves in the sun. I shadow my eyelids with black stuff and am astonished by the look of mystery it gives to my eyes. I hate being a woman. Vain and shallow and superficial. Tell a woman that you love her and she'll ask you to write it down, so that she can show it to her friends. But I am happy at that time of night.

Exercise 3.10

1) You have lent a friend, who has since left the area, a substantial amount of money — but now need it repaying.

    (i) Ring your friend and raise the matter (transcript of speech).

    (ii) Six weeks and several fruitless phone calls later (by which time you need the money urgently) write to your friend, again seeking repayment, and using whatever tone you consider most appropriate.

2) You are a bank manager and have a customer who has just become £100 overdrawn.

    (i) Send him a routine first letter informing him that he is overdrawn and suggesting repayment.

    (ii) Six weeks later, not only has the customer ignored your first and subsequent letters but he is now £200 overdrawn. Write an appropriate letter after reading p. 40.

For your guidance an intermediate letter is provided below.

NATIONAL PROGRESSIVE BANK LTD.

Bristol, Cornmarket Street Branch
PO Box No 5
20 Cornmarket Street
Bristol BS1 4PQ
Telephone Bristol 976244 (STD Code 0272)

Please address your
reply to the Manager

Your ref

Our ref   AMC/PRG/I

Date   4 February 1980

E L Goldberg Esq
c/o St. Chad's College
Bristol

Dear Mr Goldberg

Account Number 08384851

The payment of your cheque for £25 in favour of Technocrat
Limited has increased the overdraft on your account to £150.
This borrowing appears to be entirely without arrangement and I
must ask you to get in touch with me without delay to discuss your
proposals for repayment.

Yours sincerely

P. P. Snow

P P Snow
Assistant Manager

4 What does your writing tell people?

Handwriting

The way you dress, the way you speak, the way you behave — all these things suggest what kind of person you are. So too does your handwriting. Indeed some people believe they can work out your personality and even events in your past life just by studying how you write. See the extract that follows.

Reading beyond the lines

Interviewer Russell Harty, who has the reputation for asking odd questions, had the tables turned on him recently.

The beautiful lady called Justine asked him: 'Have you ever done anything to your left leg?'

'Yes, I have as a matter of fact,' he replied, sounding shaken if not completely off-balance. 'It's shorter than the right one.'

Justine hadn't seen Russell stand, let alone walk. The secret was in his handwriting. Australian-born Justine is a graphologist, the niece of A. Henry Silver, one of the pioneers of the science, and she made the intriguing revelation on a mid-week radio chat show that Russell Harty chairs.

And I know how she did it because a couple of years ago she surprised me in a similar manner. I had damaged a knee ligament and it actually showed in my signature at the time. There was a slight twist in the way I wrote the capital 'E' of my first name. As the knee improved my signature straightened out.

'Russell's give-away was the break in the 'Y' loop at the end of his name', Justine told me. 'My uncle first demonstrated this technique from a signature of a divorced friend of mine. She included her previous married name in the middle and there was a break near the top of the first letter. "Were you injured on the chin during your previous marriage? he asked her. She had been. A honeymoon ski-ing accident left her with a virtually invisible scar under the point of her chin.'

It's amazing how revealing graphology can be. Particularly in the case of one you'd imagined to be so totally hale . . . and Harty.

(from an article in *TV Times* by Ed Stewart)

This is arguable. What is less arguable is that clear, readable handwriting is an asset — whether you are taking an examination, applying for a job, or just leaving a note for the milkman. As the passage 'Wronged by how you write' (pp. 42-3) shows, for instance, teachers and examiners tend to give higher marks for 'good' handwriting. And when employers are considering hundreds of application forms for a few jobs, can you blame them if they tend to concentrate on the application forms that are clearly written?

In the same sort of way it matters how accurate your punctuation and spelling are. Some people, fairly or not, take these to be indicators of intelligence and education, and will judge you accordingly. Often (as in examinations, job application forms or letters) you are not there in person — so all the other person has to go on is your writing. Will it stand the test? Is it clear and accurate?

If not, some revision should help. The material that follows is intended to help you write more accurately — and thus give people a better impression of you (and perhaps give you a better impression of yourself!). A major problem is when people write as they would speak. As Chapter 1 shows, written and spoken English are often very different.

So, take your time over the material that follows, and don't stop until you are sure you have mastered it. You will not have been wasting your time!

Exercise 4.1

Read the extract that follows. Then discuss:

1) what 'good' handwriting is,

2) how your own handwriting rates (look back at recent exercises and essays for examples),

3) whether you were surprised to discover how important handwriting could be.

Wronged by how you write

The handwriting of school children could spell the difference between success and failure in crucial public examinations according to research carried out at the Open University.

In a study by Dennis Briggs of the Faculty of Educational Studies, essays written in five different styles attracted different marks.

Two of the handwriting samples proved so unpopular that the candidate would probably have failed the examination. 'The finding suggests that there is a borderline zone within examination marking activity where how the essay is written may be almost as critical as the essay content,' said Mr Briggs.

Five essays were chosen from a CSE English Language paper sat in 1977. This particular examination was double-marked with the second examiner unaware of the marks of the first marker. The five scripts chosen were the ones which showed the biggest disparity in marks between the two markers. Mr Briggs then copied out the essays in three different styles. Two of his children, then aged 17 and 15, copied the essays in their writing styles which had both been the subject of continual criticism at school.

All the script markers were practising teachers who were told that the effectiveness of double marking was being checked. An identical essay would have received anything from a GCE grade to a CSE grade. 'It looks very much that the 16-year-old who can present an essay one way will do better, perhaps much better, than a friend who presents exactly the same literary standard but does not or cannot make it look so attractive,' said Mr Briggs.

The research is published in *Educational Review*, Vol. 32 No. 2, 1980.

(from *The Guardian*)

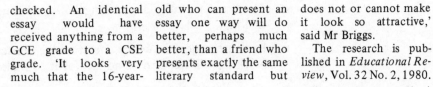

Punctuation: does it really matter?

- Look at this sentence. What does it mean?

The lecturer said the student is wasting his time.

Does it mean:

'The lecturer', said the student, 'is wasting his time'.

Or does it mean:

The lecturer said, 'The student is wasting his time'.

The words used are exactly the same in both sentences, but the meaning is quite different. What made the difference was the punctuation. So punctuation matters because it can affect meaning.

- Look at these two extracts from Examiners' Reports.

(*a*) From a report on the AEB English Language O-level Paper in 1978:

Examiners deplored most frequently the inability of candidates to write properly punctuated sentences, commas being used where full stops were needed and vice versa.

(*b*) From a report on the JMB English Literature A-level Paper in 1978:

Once again punctuation proved to be the single greatest cause of obscurity. Commas for full stops and misuse of the apostrophe were major contributions to this confusion.

Different Examining Boards, different levels, and different types of English, but they were agreed on one point — the need for good punctuation.

- 'If a job's worth doing it's worth doing well.'

What do you think?

Sentences

- Each sentence, of course, starts with a capital letter and finishes with a full stop — like this one.

43

- There are no rules about length — a sentence can be either short or long.

- Each sentence, however, must make sense standing on its own. Nothing will need to be added for it to make sense.

- As a check, then, each sentence must have a subject (someone who, or something which, is doing something) and a verb (usually what is being done).

- When reading aloud you will usually pause for breath at the end of a sentence, when you see the full stop. The pause should make sense. As a rough guide, then, when you have made one point it is time for a pause (when reading aloud) or a full stop (when writing) before you start another point.

- An exception to the two paragraphs is when two or more short sentences are combined by a conjunction (linking word) to make one longer sentence. Common conjunctions are *and*, *but*, *although*, and *however* — e.g.

  (i) He went to his room. He opened the drawer. (two short sentences)
  He went to his room *and* opened the drawer. (one longer sentence)

  (ii) He is old. He is still very fit. (two short sentences)
  Although he is old, he is still very fit. (one longer sentence)

- As another check, look at each paragraph you write. If the whole paragraph has only one or two sentences as you have punctuated it — look again — it will probably need breaking up into more sentences.

Exercise 4.2

Read the following extract and check how each sentence works.*

Now he noticed that the sky had grown much darker. The rain was heavier every second, pressing down as if the earth had to be flooded before nightfall. The oaks ahead blurred and the ground drummed. He began to run. As he ran he heard a deeper sound running with him. He whirled round. The horse was in the middle of the clearing. It might have been running to get out of the terrific rain except that it was coming for him, scattering clay and stones, with an immensely supple and powerful action. He let out a tearing roar and threw the stone in his right hand. The result was instantaneous. Whether at the roar or at the stone the horse reared as if against a wall and shied to the left.

(from 'The Rain Horse' by Ted Hughes in *Modern Short Stories*, ed. Jim Hunter)

Full stops (.)

- Used to end sentences (see 'Sentences' section above).

*It may help to read the passage aloud, pausing deliberately at each full stop.

- Used to show abbreviations.

Examples include:

e.g., i.e., Dr., Mr., B.B.C., U.S.A.

However, there is a tendency nowadays to omit full stops in abbreviations, particularly between capitals. Your television screen refers to ITN for Independent Television News (not I.T.N.) and just below in this book we write BEC (not B.E.C.) when referring to the Business Education Council.

Commas (,)

- They are used to show the reader that you want him to *pause* in order to make sense of the passage.

- But the pause is *not* as great or important as a full stop.

- Commas sometimes act like brackets: they go on either side of a phrase which could be left out without changing the main sense of the sentence — e.g.

Norita, now in her first year at college, is studying for the BEC National Diploma in Business Studies.

- Commas are sometimes used to *separate* the words in a list — e.g. coffee, tea, sugar, maize, cotton and many types of fruit are grown in central Uganda.

- Commas are also used to *introduce or interrupt* quotations (see 'Quotation Marks', p. 47) — e.g.

The young man protested, 'This is not my wife'.
'This', the young man protested, 'is not my wife'.

- Commas are also used to separate *different units of time or space* — e.g.

2 metres, 50 centimetres.
four hours, twenty minutes.

Exercise 4.3

Insert the necessary commas in the following:

1) On a bright sunny afternoon in March 1959 Robert Foster a young scientist nearly killed himself by holding his breath under-water for thirteen minutes forty two and a half seconds a world record which still stands.

2) 'Some people are taking pictures of war and pollution' she says 'and it's very important for people to do this. But *my* photographs are not like that. Nature happiness beauty — people need those things too'.

3) The Rolls-Royce Camargue the world's most expensive production car has a V8 3528 cc engine automatic transmission a top speed of 120 miles per hour and an urban fuel consumption of 10 miles per gallon.

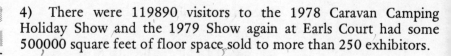

4) There were 119890 visitors to the 1978 Caravan Camping Holiday Show and the 1979 Show again at Earls Court had some 500000 square feet of floor space sold to more than 250 exhibitors.

Colons (:)

Colons are not used so much today, but they are still useful for two purposes:

- Before *announcing* a list of items or sentences. This is how it is used after the word 'purposes' above.

  'We will need the following items: bread, milk and sugar' is another example.

- To *introduce* a long quotation (instead of the usual comma) — e.g.

  Confucius said: 'Do not despise the snake because it has no horns. For who knows, one day it may become a dragon!'

Semicolons (;)

Semicolons have two main uses:

- Separating *items* in a complicated list. Consider the following sentence:

  The following extra people came: Terry, John's friend; Alice, Jane's friend; and Grandma, who wouldn't be left at home.

  Each semicolon is needed to separate off a person because we have already used a comma when describing each person. If we only used a comma, there might be *five* extra people, not three (can you see why?).

- Separating sentences which are *linked*. It is not strictly correct to write:

  I am a man, you are a woman.

  We can simply write:

  I am a man. You are a woman.

  However, if we want to suggest a connection between these sentences or a contrast, we could write:

  I am a man; you are a woman.

Apostrophes (')

- These often show *possession or belonging* — e.g.

  the doctor's car, my friend's book, the cat's tail, an elephant's memory.

- If the objects belong to several people or things (i.e. their *owners* are plural not singular) then the apostrophe comes after the s (. . . s' instead of 's) — e.g.

  The magazines' editors, the girls' opinions, the secretaries' typewriters.

- The other major use of the apostrophe is to show where a part of a word has been left out, usually in more casual English — e.g.

  could not shortens to *couldn't*
  we are shortens to *we're*
  I will or *I shall* shortens to *I'll*

- To form the plural of single letters or figures 's is sometimes used to avoid confusion — e.g.

  Do you spell your name with two t's?
  There are ten 6's in sixty.

Exercise
4.4

Insert apostrophes where necessary in the following:

1) Ill see you at Marys next Wednesday

2) Shes going to her friends brothers villa for her holiday

3) Well call the doctors if you havent time

4) The secretaries typewriters all needed cleaning

5) Whats the new secretarys name?

6) Im not sure yet whos going to Peters sisters party.

Quotation marks (' ' or " ")

"What are you after? Open the door," he said.   1
"We shan't — not till you've chosen!" said Muriel.   2
"Chosen what?" he said.   3
"Chosen the one you're going to marry," she replied.   4
He hesitated a moment.   5
"Open the blasted door," he said, "and get back to your senses." 6
He spoke with official authority.   7
"You've got to choose," cried the girls.   8
"Come on!" cried Annie, looking him in the eye. "Come on! Come 9
on!"   10

(from 'Tickets, Please' by D H Lawrence in *Modern Short Stories*,
ed. Jim Hunter)

- Quotation marks go round *all the words actually spoken*, enclosing them thus: ". . ."

- Start *a new line* when another person starts speaking.

- The first word spoken starts with a *capital letter.*

- Only put a full stop at the end of the words spoken if they are also the last words of the sentence (as in line 6 in the passage quoted).

- If the sentence continues after the last words spoken (as in the first four lines of the passage above) only put a comma, or, if necessary, a question mark or exclamation mark, after the last word spoken and before the last pair of quotation marks (").

- Where what is being said is interrupted halfway through a sentence by some such phrase as *he said*, continue the second part of the sentence being quoted with quotation marks (") and give the next word a small first letter, *not* a capital letter, to show it is all part of the original sentence (e.g. line 6 above). (Where what is being said after is a new sentence you will, of course, start it with a capital letter, e.g. line 9 above.)

- When using quotation marks you may use either '. . .' or ". . .". It may be necessary to use both if someone speaking is quoting someone else speaking — to show who is saying what:

    'I don't understand!,' Alan confessed. 'What *did* Molly mean when she said "Expect a few surprises on Thursday"?'

    What Molly said has been put inside ". . .". The question mark denotes *Alan's* question. It comes inside the '. . .' but *not* inside the ". . .". Think about it!

- Quotation marks may be used to give stress to particular words, names of individual items, or titles of books:

    The word for this sort of action is 'lunacy'.
    Flirtatious Angela was often referred to as a 'tease'.
    I've just started reading 'Watership Down'.

    (Alternatively, in print, we could use italics, without the quotation marks: *lunacy*, *tease* and *Watership Down*.)

Exercise

4.5

1) Punctuate the following sentence using commas, semi-colons, two colons and quotation marks:

The lecturer said to his English class Here are your Mock Results Sylvester and Gihad got As Tony Sharon and Mark got Bs and everyone else got a C

A possible answer is given at the end of the chapter -- but don't look until you've had a go!

2) Now punctuate the following:

What vengeance can you mean asked my father in increasing amazement I mean to decapitate the monster he answered and his clenched hand was at the same moment raised as if it were grasping the handle of an axe what exclaimed my father more than ever bewildered to strike her head off cut her head off cut her head off aye with a hatchet with a spade or with anything that can cleave through her murderous throat

(from *Carmilla* by J. Sheridan Le Fanu)

(You will have to do more than simply add quotation marks!)

Direct speech versus indirect or reported speech

- Direct speech consists of the words actually spoken and is usually indicated by quotation marks around it (" ... "), e.g. a conversation between a shop assistant and a customer:

"Could I have a copy of *Zig Zag* magazine please."

"I'm sorry, it hasn't come yet. I'll save you a copy when it does, though."

(Here we have the actual words of the speakers, i.e. *direct speech*.)

- If the general idea of what was said (but not the exact words) is related by someone else, then we have indirect or reported speech. There are no quotation marks and the word 'that' usually precedes the reporting. All present tense verbs are changed to the past tense. Thus the conversation above, in indirect speech, would become:

A customer asked the shop assistant for a copy of *Zig Zag* magazine. The shop assistant replied he was sorry but the magazine hadn't arrived. He would, however, save a copy when one arrived.

Exercise 4.6

Which of the following are direct and which indirect speech?

1) Dr Johnson said, "The man who is tired of London is tired of life."

2) The Prime Minister admitted that unemployment had risen again.

3) The Leader of the Opposition said he did not accept the government's arguments.

4) She said, "What will be, will be."

5) She said that what would happen would happen.

Question mark (?)

- This is used at the end of a *direct* question — either to someone else as indicated by quotation marks (" ... ") or to the reader (so no quotation marks) — e.g.

'Where are you going for lunch?' she asked.
Where are you going for lunch? (a note on my desk)

- It is *not* used after an *indirect* question (i.e. one in indirect speech) — e.g.

  She asked me where I was going for lunch.

- Nor is it used after a *request*, although the request may be disguised as a question — e.g.

  Will you please send me a copy of the new catalogue.

Spelling: how important is it?

Exercise 4.7

Read the following sentences. What mistakes have been made?

1) It would be a good idea if more of our policemen were trained in the marital arts.

2) Two big men, dressed smartly in three-piece suites . . .

3) We request your presents at the meeting.

4) His clothes are all at the pornshop.

The spelling mistakes you make as a student, like the ones above, sometimes amuse your English teacher. More often, however, they will irritate or annoy him (especially if they are common words, or mistakes he's pointed out to you before) . . .

. . . as well as examiners, employers etc.

The difficulty of teaching spelling, though, is that different students make different mistakes. Try helping yourself then. Get a little note pad. Head each page with a different letter of the alphabet. Each time you make a mistake (and not just in work for English) find out the correct spelling (you do have a dictionary don't you?) and write it up in your notebook. Test yourself regularly and try to use the corrected words in your writing. That way you can learn the spellings *you* need.

It will also help to look for *patterns* of spelling. As we saw in Chapter 1, there is no necessary connection between the way a word is pronounced and the way it is spelt. However, there are *some* connections, otherwise spelling would be even more difficult. As an example look for connections between spelling and pronunciation in the following groups:

A		B	C			
hop	hope	gnat	hat	heart	hate	
not	note	reign	cat	cart	cater	
rob	robe	resign	mat	martin	mate	
hat	hate	phlegm	back	bark	bake	
fat	fate	sign	lack	lark	lake	lace
mat	mate	feign	mac	mark	make	mace
man	mane		pack	park		pace
Sam	same		struck	stalk	stake	
plan	plane		tack	talk	take	
rime	time		wack	walk	wake	
bit	bite					
kit	kite					

Vocabulary: how many words do you know?

Exercise
4.8

You need a sheet of paper or a pencil.

Beginning at word Number 1, read through the words of the first test on p. 52 in the order numbered. As you come to a word you do not know, write the number of the word on your sheet of paper. Carry on in this way until you have ten numbers on your sheet. At that point *stop*, whether or not you know the next word. That is to say, you read through the test until you have met ten words that you do not know the meaning of. Now you must show that you really do know the words you claimed to know. It is enough if you show that you can give a correct meaning to the last five words you claimed to know — that is, the last five words whose numbers you did not write down. You can do this in each case by making a small sketch to illustrate the meaning, by writing about the meaning, or by showing in a sentence how the word is used.

Repeat this process for Tests 2 and 3.

Vocabulary range

Test 1

Level 1	Level 2	Level 3	Level 4	Level 5
1. abroad	11. abandon	21. abridge	31. abhorrent	41. abscissa
2. boulder	12. ballot	22. aggregate	32. amorphous	42. badinage
3. dawdle	13. chaos	23. bivouac	33. crustacean	43. cartel
4. expedition	14. contraband	24. chronology	34. declivity	44. daemon
5. horizon	15. excavate	25. credulous	35. emaciated	45. dendrite
6. jangle	16. fatigue	26. hireling	36. fabrication	46. exordium
7. limit	17. laboratory	27. indolent	37. galaxy	47. inchoate
8. pattern	18. manual	28. nomadic	38. heretical	48. moraine
9. rate	19. purchase	29. accidental	39. igneous	49. rubric
10. stroke	20. shuttle	30. somnambulism	40. nomenclature	50. soutane

Test 2

Level 1	Level 2	Level 3	Level 4	Level 5
1. abbey	11. accelerate	21. acrid	31. baroque	41. abreast
2. abundance	12. aquatic	22. aftermath	32. cabal	42. atavistic
3. boast	13. celebrity	23. centrifugal	33. Charybdis	43. claque
4. convenient	14. identical	24. circuitous	34. dorsal	44. dharma
5. decimal	15. latitude	25. faction	35. ephemeral	45. flagellum
6. happiness	16. martial	26. interim	36. fiscal	46. gerrymander
7. invisible	17. rotary	27. nautical	37. invective	47. haptic
8. somersault	18. teem	28. retrograde	38. lymphatic	48. imbroglio
9. torpedo	19. terminate	29. splice	39. mandible	49. janissary
10. undergrowth	20. veteran	30. vehement	40. palliative	50. phrenetic

Test 3

Level 1	Level 2	Level 3	Level 4	Level 5
1. absence	11. abode	21. admit	31. acquiesce	41. accidie
2. agriculture	12. barricade	22. alabaster	32. agrarian	42. burette
3. blizzard	13. bulletin	23. bigotry	33. bullion	43. coruscate
4. crescent	14. climax	24. circumvent	34. clandestine	44. contumely
5. downpour	15. crouch	25. culminate	35. desultory	45. desuetude
6. fragment	16. export	26. fallacious	36. eradicate	46. frustum
7. hemisphere	17. flimsy	27. mediocre	37. fluted	47. haulm
8. reach	18. hospitality	28. nutritious	38. homogeneous	48. imago
9. sheaf	19. longitude	29. parry	39. larynx	49. mandragora
10. triangle	20. rustic	30. rancour	40. overt	50. normative

(from *Standard Literacy Tests* by Hunter Diack)

So — how many words *do* you know?

The mark in each test is the number of words known in that test up to the tenth unknown word. The total vocabulary is the average score in three tests multiplied by 600, e.g. average score 25 = total vocabulary $25 \times 600 = 15,000$ words. You may find this hard to believe but extensive tests have shown this to be a very accurate estimate of how many words a person knows. So, multiply your average score (i.e. Total over 3 tests ÷ 3) by 600, to find out how many words you know. This exercise will probably show you both how much you know already, and also how much more you could learn!

Increasing your vocabulary

The best way to increase your vocabulary is by wide reading. That way you will not only meet new words but also see how words can have different meanings, depending on the context — just think how many meanings a simple word like *run* can have, for instance. The more new words you come across, the more you come across them, and the more ways you find to use them yourself, the more your *active* vocabulary will grow.

The next section, incidentally, deals with prefixes. They are included as useful vocabulary builders, since knowing prefixes can make it easier to remember words you come across and to work out what they mean.

Prefixes: some common examples

Copy the following and fill in the blank spaces. Where the blank space is for examples try to give at least three.

Prefix	Meaning	Examples
anti-	against, opposed to	anticlimax anticlockwise antiseptic
auto-		autobiography automatic automobile
	not	dislike disused disappear
mis-	wrongly, badly	
pre-	before	
	many	polygamous (having more than one husband or wife) polygon
		p.m. (post meridiem) p.s. (postscript) post mortem postgraduate
		telephone television telescope
		transatlantic transcontinental transmit transfer
		unfortunate unforgettable unforgivable

Now, having done this, start to draw up your own list, taking one prefix a day, and finding as many examples as possible. In a few weeks your vocabulary will increase considerably.

Who are you writing to?

The way we write depends on three things in particular:

- who we are writing to
- why we are writing
- how people normally write in this situation
  (probably how they have been taught to write in this situation).

These three factors will affect *how much* we write, *how we set it out*, *what words we use, what tone and register* (e.g. formal or informal), and perhaps even *how neatly* we write and what kind of pen or pencil we use.

Exercise 4.10

Read the following questions and ask yourself how different answers would affect the points we have mentioned above.

1) How old is your reader — in relation to you?

2) What sex is your reader?

3) Is there just one reader — or many?

4) How well do you know the reader(s)?
(e.g. boyfriend or girlfriend/close friend/friend/family/relative/colleague/acquaintance/friend of friend/stranger).

5) What status is your reader — in relation to you?

6) What nationality is your reader?

7) How much do you know about your reader?

8) How much does your reader know about you?

All these should affect the form and language you use.

Exercise 4.11

You are not able to see the following people in time so have to leave a note/message. Apply what you have learnt from discussing 1–8 above:

1) Your mother: tell her you have gone out with friends and will be back late. (She's the worrying kind, incidentally.)

2) Your form teacher/personal tutor: explain you are going into hospital for a few days so will be away from school/college.

3) The new milkman: he left too much milk yesterday, so you will need less today and the normal amount from tomorrow onwards.

55

Why are you writing anyway?

This question can mean two things. If it means what are you trying to communicate, the answer will probably lie in one of the following suggestions (i.e. to inform, persuade, maintain relations etc.).

Would the words you would choose vary, depending on your purpose? Give some examples of this.

If it means why are you using writing rather than any other medium of communication (e.g. talking) then the answer will normally be something along these lines:

- *Writing is permanent* (so that you can check it later, e.g. a contract).

- *Writing is cheap and space-saving* (e.g. you can store lecture notes on tape but it is a more expensive and bulky method than writing them on a sheet of paper).

- *Writing enables you to communicate without being there in person* (from a note left for the milkman to a book written by someone who could never communicate personally with all his readers otherwise).

Exercise 4.12

From the information above and elsewhere in the book, together with your own knowledge and experience, draw up a chart which shows visually:

1) Possible mediums of communication.

2) The value of each (bearing in mind e.g. accuracy, cost, effectiveness etc.).

Then, working from this, draw up a list of situations where writing will be the best means of communication, seeing who can suggest most situations.

Answer to Exercise 4.5, p. 48

The lecturer said to his English class: 'Here are your Mock Results: Sylvester and Gihad got A's; Tony, Sharon and Mark got B's; and everyone else got a C.'

5   Types of writing

'I answered an ad that said: "Ideal job — all you do is watch television all day".'

What time is it?

How can I increase my chances of surviving a plane crash?

How do I get to Dover Road?

What exactly is a polytechnic?

How much is the small size?

If I go fell walking what should I take with me?

Unless you're a vegetable there'll be times in your life when you want to find things out — even if it's just the time of the next bus or train. A lot of things you can just ask. You can ask a complete stranger what the time is and have a good chance of an accurate reply. But some things even your friends or family might not know. Look at the questions above. How would you find the answers?

57

Exercise 5.1

Now look at the passage below. Does it help you answer the second question?

There is a simple drill in an emergency which much improves your chance of survival. First, remove any sharp or metal objects from your pockets; a pen or comb can cause serious injury on impact. Put them in the seat pockets in front of you. Make sure the seat belt is really tight, and the seat upright. Take off tie and spectacles. Put your feet flat on the floor, not under your seat or the one in front. The seat could collapse and trap you. Work out exactly what escape route you are going to use, and make sure you have an alternative should the first be impossible for any reason.

When the crash is imminent, try to cover your head with a rug or pillow. Put your arms, with fingers interlocked, over your neck and push your face into your knees, keeping your feet straight down. The aircraft will probably hit more than once in the crash, so don't move from the braced position until the aircraft has stopped. When it has definitely done so, undo your belt and get out of the plane, fast. Once out, run away from it as fast as you can in case it explodes. Do not take any possessions with you, briefcase, cameras, anything. Delay kills.

Obey the crew, but never expect them to rescue you. Rescue yourself. Thus you should work out for yourself how to operate emergency exits, ensure your legs are not trapped, minimise the odds of being knocked unconscious by protecting your head. Never ever inflate a lifejacket inside an aircraft. It will jam you in the exit, stopping your escape and that of the other passengers.

Above all, the wise passenger knows that he can make it if he does not panic. Most accidents are on take-off and landing, where the speed is not great and where impact itself is usually survivable. It is not the crash in an aircrash that kills, but suffocation or poisoning later. The wise passenger, anticipating a crash, remembers: 'Impact does not kill. Fumes and fire do'.

As a rule of thumb he has 60 seconds to get out.

(from *Airport International* by Brian Moynahan)

As the question was a fairly specialised one it needed fairly specialised information to answer it. For anything else a little bit out of the ordinary you'll probably need to check with a specialist book, guide or instruction manual. Asking people probably won't be enough.

However, specialised information can be a problem. In particular it can be difficult to follow — especially if it uses specialist terms. How much sense does the following piece of information make, for instance (for you, anyway)?

The behaviour of 'absorption currents' in polyethylene was observed to be similar to that of polypropylene (Das Gupta and Joyner 1976) except that the onset of a quasi-steadystate conduction current in the charging transients occurred at earlier times and lower temperature and field in the present case. As in the case of polypropylene, the 'absorption current' in polyethylene also showed a marked increase with temperature above 273 K in comparison with its behaviour below it. The observed magnitude of n in the low-temperature range of 113–273 K and the absence of any thickness dependence and any significant electrode material effect will rule out tunnelling (Wintle 1973), electrode polarisation (Macdonald 1971) and charge-injection-forming trapped space charge (Walden 1972, Wintle 1974) as possible mechanisms for 'absorption currents'.

(from *Journal of Physics* D: *Applied Physics*)

Exercise 5.2

Now, have a look at the passages that follow. How well do they put over their information? To help you here are a few questions to consider:

1) Is there one big block of information, or is it broken up into separate points? (and which is easier to follow?).

2) Is the language easy to follow?
(e.g. not too many technical terms, or complicated sentences.)

3) Is there variety of presentation, to attract and keep your interest?
(e.g. pictures, different sizes and types of print, numbered points etc.)

4) Are some points more memorable because of the way they're expressed? (which, and why?).

5) Does the passage seem to be written *to you*? How personal is the approach?

6) How *relevant* is the information to you? Could you go out and use it — *now/next week/next year/ever*?

7) So far as you can judge, how accurate is the information?

8) After reading each piece do you feel like following the advice?
(If so, why? If not, why not?)

9) Does it help to be told *why* you should do something — or do you just prefer to be told what to do?

10) Does the *amount* of information you're given affect your response?

11) If things need to be done in a definite order, is the order clearly stated and easy to follow?

12) If some points are more important than others, is it clear what the order of importance is?

(*a*) Of course, we all have binges . . . and they certainly affect eye beauty. Quickest way to get rid of hangover-bleary eyes is to drink lots of water and lemon juice (to replace Vitamin C) and to bathe your eyes with cold tea or lukewarm water.

(Part of an article on eye care in a woman's magazine)

(*b*)

FELL WALKERS!
READ THIS
and live a little longer . . .

British mountains can be killers if proper care is not taken. The following notes cover the **minimum** precautions if you want to avoid getting hurt or lost, and so inconveniencing or endangering others as well as yourselves.

CLOTHING.   This should be colourful, warm, windproof and water-proof. Wear boots with nails or moulded rubber soles, not shoes, plimsolls, or gum-boots. Take a woollen cap and a spare jersey; it is always colder on the tops.

FOOD. **In addition** to the usual sandwiches take chocolate, dates, mint cake or similar sweet things which restore energy quickly. If you don't need them yourself, someone else may.

EQUIPMENT.   This **must** include map, compass, and at least one reliable watch in the party. A whistle and torch (a series of six blasts or flashes repeated at minute intervals signal an emergency) and, in winter conditions, an ice-axe and survival bag are **essential.**

COMPANY. Don't go alone, and make sure party leaders are experienced. Take special care of the youngest and weakest in dangerous places.

(By courtesy of the Lake District Mountain Accidents Association)

(*c*) *An apple a day keeps the doctor away.*

(Anon)

(*d*) SUNTAN PREPARATIONS. With more knowledge available about the effects of the sun's rays on the skin, there is no excuse for anybody but the careless few to burn in the sun. Even highly-sensitive redheads can now prevent their skin from turning a painful lobster pink, with sun-block preparations, such as those made by Clinique or Elizabeth Arden.

Most well-known suntan preparations, such as Ambre Solaire, Bergasol, Eversun, Hawaiian Tropic and Soltan, have a Sun Protection Factor, or SPF, printed on the pack. This will tell you how long you can safely stay in sun when using the product. For example, if you normally burn after 10 minutes exposure without any suntan preparation, a product with an SPF rating of 6 would allow you to extend your sunning time to 60 minutes. Basically, the higher the SPF number, the longer you'll be protected against harmful rays.

Always start with a high protection factor, usually the creams rather than oils, in order to let your skin become accustomed to the sun.

Certain areas of the body will always need more protection, even if you are one of the lucky ones and tan very easily. The nose, cheekbones, eyelids, lips, collarbones, elbows, knees, shins and feet are the most vulnerable areas, so always use a high-protection cream or a specially-formulated sunblock product, such as Eversun Lip Protection Stick, at 84p.

Suntan preparations should be applied about every two hours and always after swimming. An exception is Aquasun by Roche, which is water-resistant and need be applied only about twice a day. Nevertheless, local conditions should be taken into consideration. For example, the nearer the Equator you go, the stronger the sun's rays. Even on hazy or cloudy days, 80 per cent of the sun's rays may reach the Earth. Hiding under umbrellas without protection is no use, since ultra-violet rays reflect from white buildings, concrete pavements, the sand and the sea, and still inflict skin damage.

(from *TV Times*)

(e) **BE YOUR OWN BOSS**

You don't have to work for someone else. You could try working for yourself. It can be hard work. You'd have to think it out first. This page gives you a start.

WHAT CAN YOU DO?

Here are some ideas: babysitting, window cleaning, car cleaning, push-bike repairs, painting and decorating, cleaning people's houses, making and selling toys, clothes or candles, gardening.

There are plenty of other ideas. Talk it over with friends or family. If you can come up with something unusual, all the better!

GETTING ORGANISED

● Find out if people want what you're offering.

'I thought I'd try window cleaning. I went calling, and found people who said "Yes".'

'I advertised in a shop window, "Bike repairs — ring 27914". I had 10 calls in 2 days.'

● Do you need equipment? Can you afford it? (e.g. window cleaners need a ladder, a bike, two buckets, sponge, leather, detergent.)

- You may need a permit. Ask the Citizens' Advice Bureau.

- Where will you advertise — local paper? — shop windows? — knocking on doors? Spreading the word by family and friends?

- Can people phone you? If not, how will they contact you? By letter? Calling on you?

- Will you need to get insurance, in case you hurt yourself or break something?

HOW MUCH SHOULD YOU CHARGE?

You'll need to charge for anything you need to buy to do the job, and then charge for your time. Work out an hourly rate for yourself. Keep invoices (bills) for things you have bought. Give your customers a bill saying how much you have spent on materials and how much you're charging for your labour.

SOCIAL SECURITY

You may not earn much at first. You can still claim Social Security, but if you earn more than £4 a week, they will take it off your benefit.

JOHN'S STORY

John Hughes (18) left school and couldn't find a job. Friends of his parents asked him to paint the outside of their house. He did it so well that he was asked to paint someone else's house, and so it went on. At the moment he's painting a factory.

John: 'I went to the local paint shop and told them what I was doing, and they said that if I bought more than a certain amount of stuff from them they would give me a trade discount.'

How do you find work?

John: I just keep my ears and eyes open. My mum and dad tell their friends who tell their friends and so on. I also talk to people in pubs. Times when I haven't found it — well I've been lucky. It hasn't been for long. You're ready for that anyway.

(from the *Roadshow Handbook*)

(*f*) **Essay technique on a set book for English Literature**

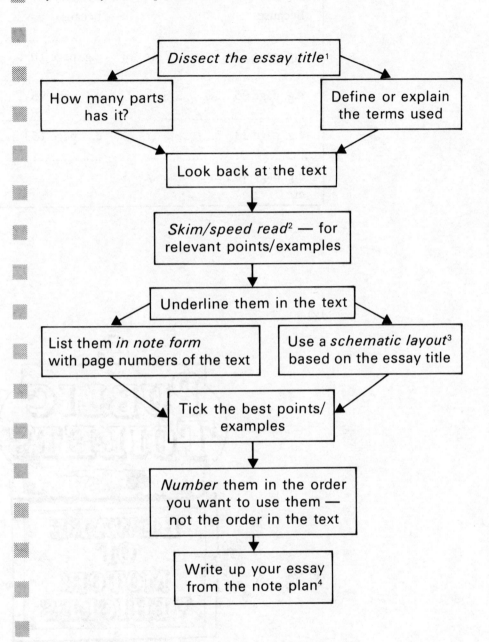

Notes. 1 First be clear what you are looking for.
2 Don't waste time — ignore anything else!
3 Keep these notes — they will be excellent for revision.
4 The final note plan, for a typical essay along the lines of, '_____, To what extent do you agree with this statement? would probably look something like this:

Agree			Disagree		
because			because		
....			....		
e.g. page 3	✓	4	e.g. page 10	✓	1
....			....		
e.g. page 25			e.g. page 98		
....			....		
e.g. page 33	✓	3	e.g. page 153	✓	2
....			....		
e.g. page 48	✓	5			
etc.					

(g)

By now you should have a fair idea about what makes a good piece of informative writing. Try these exercises and see:

Exercise 5.3

1) Prepare a clear and interesting guide to:
   (i) a sport or indoor game which is not well known (as a test, when it is written your friends who do not know the sport or game should be able to play it just by following the guide);
   (ii) a useful skill, hobby or activity.

2) Prepare a short *instruction manual* on how to work a machine you are familiar with (a motorbike, sewing machine, lawn mower, washing machine, typewriter etc.) for someone who knows nothing about one.

3) Prepare a short handbook of useful information for someone who is leaving home for the first time to live on his (or her) own. (Assume he or she will be living in the same area.)

4) Prepare a school or college handbook, introducing the place to new students.

Descriptive writing

Use of words

Read the following passage, by the South African writer Alex la Guma.

Michael Adonis turned into the entrance of a tall narrow tenement where he lived. The floor of the entrance was flagged with white and black slabs in the pattern of a draught-board, but the tramp of untold feet and the accumulation of dust and grease and ash had blurred the squares so that now it had taken on the appearance of a kind of loathsome skin disease. A row of dustbins lined one side of the entrance and exhaled the smell of rotten fruit, stale food, stagnant water and general decay. A cat, the colour of dishwater, was trying to paw the remains of a fish-head from one of the bins.

She came down and stood on the first step, smiling at him and showing the gap in the top row of her teeth. She had a heavy mouth, smeared blood-red with greasy lipstick, so that it looked stark as a wound in her dark face. Her coarse wiry hair was tied at the back with a scrap of soiled ribbon in the parody of a ponytail, and under the blouse and skirt her body was insignificant. She was wearing new yellow leather flat-heeled pumps that gave the impression of something expensive abandoned on a junk heap.

(from *A Walk in the Night* by Alex la Guma)

Exercise 5.4

Would you like to live in the place he describes? Would you be flattered if you were described as the girl is described? If not:

1) List the words which you feel give an unfavourable impression. Is there any connection between these words?

65

2) Now rewrite the passage to give the opposite picture — of a charming and attractive location and person.

Do this by changing the words you have listed. Where possible change the details as little as possible, just the impressions (e.g. most qualities can be seen two ways).

A person may seem *generous* to his friends but *spendthrift* to his wife: the same quality viewed two ways. So, in the passage, the girl's 'insignificant' body could be described, more attractively, as 'slim' (without altering her actual appearance we have altered the words to give a different impression). This may not always be possible, of course. We may have for example to replace 'dustbins' by 'flowers', but alter as little as possible otherwise.

Pen portraits

Here is a pen portrait of the main character of Alan Sillitoe's short story 'Uncle Ernest'.

A middle aged man wearing a dirty raincoat, who badly needed a shave and looked as though he hadn't shaved for a month, came out of a public lavatory with a cloth bag of tools folded beneath his arm. Standing for a moment on the edge of the pavement to adjust his cap — the cleanest thing about him — he looked casually to the left and right and, when the traffic flow had eased off, crossed the road. His name and his trade were always spoken of in one breath: Ernest Brown the upholsterer. Every night before returning to his lodgings he left the bag of tools for safety with a man who looked after the public lavatory near the town centre, for he felt there was a risk of them being lost or stolen should he take them back to his room, and if such a thing were to happen his living would be gone.

A   A pen portrait nearly always contains a physical description of a subject. There is no need, however, to describe every detail of the person. What kind of shoes did Ernest Brown wear? What was his walk like? You are not given this precise information in the extract but you could certainly feel confident about answering these questions.

B   The reason for this is that the writer has carefully *selected* the details he has used. The fact that Ernest was wearing a dirty raincoat and that he needed a shave is enough for us to imagine the details of his clothing and appearance. What details help in suggesting how Ernest might walk?

C   From this short extract we know that Ernest Brown was poor, lonely, unhappy, badly organised, working class; we know that he is distrustful of others and not very resourceful; and we could probably make a good guess as to the opinions he might hold on a whole range of subjects.

D It is far better to suggest than to describe. The reason why we know so much about Ernest Brown is that the details the writer has given us work upon our suggestibility and we then tend to fill in the rest of the picture for ourselves. But the details given must have this ability to suggest. If Sillitoe had simply said that Ernest's family were all dead and that he lived in lodgings, we would have had little more than these bits of information. By telling us about his habit of leaving his tools in the public lavatory he excites our imagination and convinces us of the uniqueness of this man.

Exercise 5.5

Using the technique of *selected* detail, write four pen portraits:

1) One of a young woman or girl.
2) One of an old woman.
3) One of a young man or boy.
4) One of an old man.

(If you wish, you may base these on people you know.)

Some general points

Exercise 5.6

Read this passage:

Glasgow Corporation Slaughter House

The slaughter-house was inside a huge area, surrounded by buff coloured walls. This area, which was all roofed-in, comprised the cattle market where the pigs, sheep and cattle awaited sale and slaughter, the slaughter-house, where the animals were killed and dressed, and the meat market where the animals, now transformed into beef, pork and mutton, were sold to the butchers. Inside this place on a Wednesday afternoon, which was market day, there was always a welter of activity; big livestock trucks backing into the various entrances and disgorging their big boots, labourers with their dungarees beginning to shine and darken with grease and coagulated blood, white-coated salesmen who were cutting, pinching and slapping at the hanging meat; there were swinging slabs of meat which hung from cambrels fixed to an overhead trolley and which were sliding down from the slaughter-house to be lost in the rows of meat hanging in the various stalls and stances; the red gape of cut meat, the yellow marbled sides of beef, the sawdust that soaked up the dripping blood from the necks of the carcases, barrowsful of day-old calves with slacked limbs and lolling heads, the pink schoolgirl complexions of the scalded pigs, droplets of red blood on the cobbles. This was the meat market.

You went up to the slaughter-house through a big lorry-filled entrance gate and underneath a tangle of lights and girders which supported the system of rails on which the cambrels hung, then right through and up a wide pass, tarmacadamed and with red glazed brick walls. In the slaughter-house itself were rows of big cubicles where the animals were dressed and flayed. Outside these rooms hung the freshly killed steaming carcases awaiting the porters who would stick a meat hook into the spaul and slide them away. There were heaps of feet being cleaned up by labourers into barrows, heaps of round manyplies, the fat stuffed fourth stomach of the ox, which the killers would skite out of their rooms like curling stones, slipping on the blood soaked floor, and limp hides with the hair all soaked with water and blood lying in folds amongst the other stuff. The men, all rubber-booted, walked carefully with an odd mincing gait among the pools of blood and water, among the slippery refuse, the feet, manyplies, pieces of fat and lumps of jelly-like lappered blood. In the middle of the pass barrows were being pushed up and down as the labourers collected the offal — tripes, livers, hearts, lungs, heads. And all the time the grinding of machinery, the cries of men, the clatter of iron-felloed wheels, the crack of the guns, the lowing and bellowing of the cattle and the crunch of the big heavy bodies being felled on to the concrete floor.

Mat worked in one of these slaughter-rooms. At first he had felt slight revulsion, though perhaps less so than most who started work there. It was not the shambles that caused this, however. He found it quite easy to have his arms covered up to the elbows in reeking blood, and he handled the dripping gobbets of offal and fat with no qualms. What he did dislike was the moment when the animals, the frisky wee bullocks, the quiet maternal cows, the placid indifferent bulls, had their heads tied to the stunning post, and the gun, the bolt pistol, was fired into their foreheads between the eyes. The gun cracked and the animals went down on to the floor in the same sudden moment. Like a felled ox, Mat would think. For nothing, other than the thing itself, could convey that quick loosening of the limbs as they slackened and folded under the animal and it would drop on its knees, its stomach, and its chin, all together, making an odd sound combining the slap of soft flesh and the solid but dull crunch of the padded bone as the chin bounced loosely on the concrete floor. Then the shuddering sigh and the spasm of the muscles as the animal tensed them to grip at the soft elusive life which suspired from the tiny hole in its forehead. Mat found this difficult to get used to, and with every crack and thud of a beast dropping he would ponder on the fragility of bone.

(from *The Dear Green Place* by Archie Hind)

This is a very powerful piece of descriptive writing. After reading it, you should really *know* what it would be like to visit the place. These few questions which follow are designed to draw your attention to the techniques the writer uses to achieve this description.

1) Good descriptive writing always appeals to the eye, the eye of the imagination, that is, The writer puts things in such a vivid way that we immediately 'see' what he is describing. This passage has many such examples.

Make a list of the expressions in this passage that made you vividly 'see' the thing described.

2) Similarly, good descriptive writing appeals to the ear. Although they are slightly more difficult to find, make a list of all the expressions which appeal to your ear.

3) Another technique which helps to convey the 'feel' of a place is the use of specialist words and terms. Make a list of all the words in the passage that you do not understand. Find out the meanings of them in the dictionary. Which of these words are specialised words?

4) The descriptive writer has to be very observant. He must see details and be able to represent them in an accurate way. For instance, in this passage the writer has noticed the strange walk of the men who work in the slaughter-house: 'The men, all rubber-booted, walked carefully with an odd mincing gait among the blood and water, among the slippery refuse . . .'

Write out other examples of the writer's acute observation.

We may conclude that good descriptive writing has the following features:

- It appeals to the *eye*.
- It appeals to the *ear*.
- It appeals to the other senses, too − taste, touch, smell.
- It shows the writer's knowledge of the subject − by the correct use of specialised words and terms.
- It shows the writer's keen observation.
- It is careful language. That is, every word, phrase and sentence has been carefully chosen for the maximum effectiveness.
- It arouses the reader's interest and manages to hold it.

Exercise 5.7

With these ideas in mind it is important that you now try to write a piece of descriptive prose. Write not less than 400 words describing *A Place of Activity*.

Try to convey the bustle, the action and the atmosphere. You can include descriptions of the place itself, the people there, the kind of activity, and specialised acts or movements involved and changes which occur through the day. It is important to choose a place you are familiar with.

Here are a few suggestions of bustling places which might serve as subjects for your description:
- A cafe or restaurant
- A market
- A garage
- A school
- A department store
- A boxing arena.

Write a short passage of about 500 words on one of the following topics.

1) A self-portrait.

2) Compare your journey to school/college on a delightful summer's day with the same journey on a cold unpleasant winter's day.

3) Loneliness.

4) Describe the work involved in a part-time or holiday job you have.

5) An unusual person you know.

6) A view from a high building.

7) Figures and faces.

8) The storm.

9) Happiness is _____ .

10) Describe a popular holiday spot:
   (i) early in the morning, before the crowds have arrived;
   (ii) later in the day, when it is full of people.

11) The most beautiful person/place in the world.

12) A work of art/piece of machinery that intrigued you.

Narrative writing

The report on yesterday's controversial football match in the sports pages of the newspaper; your account of what really happened at the party in a letter to a friend; Samuel Pepys' *Diary* (or anyone else's diary for that matter); many folk song and pop song lyrics; most myths, legends, fairy stories and nursery rhymes: novels and short stories: these may all seem very different in content — but they are all examples of narrative writing. They all relate to a series of events (and they don't even need to be factual to count as narrative writing — telling a story is narrative just the same).

Narrative is therefore an extremely common form of writing. As it usually follows the order of events, i.e. 'First . . . Then . . . Next . . . Finally . . .', it is easy to remember and easy to follow. Indeed, people will often slip into narrative even when it *isn't* wanted because it comes so easily. For instance, it is a common complaint of examiners that many literature students end up telling the story (i.e. narrative writing) rather than answering the questions set (e.g. analytical writing).

In one sense, then, narrative is the one type of writing you as a student should need least help with, as it is the kind that seems to come most naturally. However, it is still worth considering these three rules: normally the events described should be:

- *interesting in themselves* (if they are not, why are you writing about them?);

- *told without irrelevant sidetracking* (a stock comic character is the one who starts off telling a story but never quite gets to the end as each event sparks off some extra thought or memory which is then pursued at length);

- *told in an interesting and varied manner* (an interesting start always helps — and some sort of message or moral at the end may give the account added weight).

Exercise 5.9

Now read the passages that follow. Do they follow the three rules of narrative writing? Is there more to narrative than the three rules suggest — and if so, what?

(*a*) **Passport to paradise**

He passed the bobby without fuss,
And he passed the cart of hay,
He tried to pass a swerving bus,
And then he passed away.

(Anon)

(*b*) **An evening at home with the old-style man**

When we had finished eating I took the plates back to the kitchen. I was determined not to start washing-up, but the masculine squalor of the sink and its surroundings compelled me. Nothing had been touched since the morning before: the sink-hole was stopped with a mound of tealeaves, and there was a pile of dirty cups and saucers all over the draining board. I looked anxiously for a glass or two but there were none: my suspicions were right, he must be a secret abstainer.

When I tore myself away from it we went and sat down on the settee, and kissed in some discomfort. After a while he said that perhaps we might go up and lie on the bed, and I said that perhaps we might, so we went up to the bedroom. But it was useless. I couldn't bring myself to think about it at all.

'What's the matter?' he said, after a while. 'What's the matter with me? What have I done? Don't you want me to make love to you, Emma?'

'Not particularly,' I said, turning over and lying on my back to stare at the ceiling. 'Not particularly, to tell you the truth.'

'Why not?'

'Oh, I don't know,' I said. 'All that washing-up, and I can see that there's a button off your shirt, and I know that any minute now you're going to ask me to sew it on for you, aren't you? Be honest, tell me, you were, weren't you?'

'Well, it had crossed my mind. But not immediately, of course, not now.'

'No. After.'

'Yes, I suppose so. After.'

I started to laugh. 'Oh well,' I said. 'At least you admitted it. If you hadn't admitted it, that would have been that. Tell me, Wyndham, what makes you think that I'm better at sewing on buttons than you are?'

'Well, you're a woman. More practice.'

'You could start practising now. Then you wouldn't have to take a woman to bed with you in order to get your buttons sewn on. I'll give you a lesson.'

(from *The Garrick Year* by Margaret Drabble)

(c)   The companion

She was sitting on the rough embankment,
her cape too big for her tied on slapdash
over an odd little hat with a bobble on it,
her eyes brimming with tears of hopelessness.
An occasional butterfly floated down
fluttering warm wings onto the rails.
The clinkers under foot were deep lilac.
We got cut off from our grandmothers
while the Germans were dive-bombing the train.
Katya was her name. She was nine.
I'd no idea what I could do about her,
but doubt quickly dissolved to certainty:
I'd have to take this thing under my wing;
— girls were in some sense of the word human,
a human being couldn't be just left.
The droning in the air and the explosions
receded farther into the distance,
I touched the little girl on her elbow.
"Come on. Do you hear? What are you waiting for?"
The world was big and we were not big,
and it was tough for us to walk across it.
She had galoshes on and felt boots,
I had a pair of second-hand boots.
We formed streams and tramped across the forest;
each of my feet at every step it took
taking a smaller step inside the boot.
The child was feeble, I was certain of it.
"Boo-hoo," she'd say. "I'm tired," she'd say.
She'd tire in no time I was certain of it,
but as things turned out it was me who tired.

I growled I wasn't going any further
and sat down suddenly beside the fence.
"What's the matter with you?" she said.
"Don't be stupid! Put grass in your boots.
Do you want to eat something? Why won't you talk?
Hold this tin, this is crab.
We'll have refreshments. You small boys,
you're always pretending to be brave."
Then out I went across the prickly stubble
marching beside her in a few minutes.
Masculine pride was muttering in my mind:
I scraped together strength and I held out
for fear of what she'd say. I even whistled.
Grass was sticking out from my tattered boots.
So on and on
we walked without thinking of rest
passing craters, passing fires,
under the rocking sky of '41
tottering crazy on its smoking columns.

(Y Yevtushenko)

(d)   **Opportunity**

Opportunity
Came to my door
When I was down
On my luck
In the shape
Of an old friend
With a plan
Guaranteed

Showed me the papers
As he walked me to the car
His shoes
Finest leather
He said
You could wear this style
If you follow my advice

He owned a gun
The calibre escaped me
But I noticed
Straight away
It make me itch
Carried an address
With numbers on the back
And an L shaped
Bar of iron

What's that for
I asked my man
With eyes
Wide opened

And the knowledge in my head
And he said
Opportunity
World wide adventure
Money in the bank

We did the job
The work was so well done
No one saw us coming
Much less leave
But what I dropped
Carried my credentials
And a black and white
Shot of you and me

What's that for
I asked the cop
With eyes of innocence
And the knowledge in my head

And he said
Opportunity
World wide adventure
Let me have your hand.

(from Joan Armatrading's LP *Show Some Emotion*)

(e)   **How Spider escaped death**

Once upon a time Death was walking about the country. He was looking for victims, and as a bait, he led behind him a very fat ox. He only asked one price — that after a year had gone by the purchaser should not forget his name. If he should forget his name, then Death would carry him off. Now Spider was poor and starving with no idea where the next meal was going to come from, and of course he hastened to buy the fat ox at that price.

After Spider had bought the ox and had agreed with Death upon the price — that he must be able to repeat Death's name, Wanabéri, at the end of a year — he led the beast home in triumph. There he killed it and skinned it and cut it into pieces for the members of his family, and their time of hunger was past.

Death went on his way, and Spider called his wife and his son, and ordered them to sing this new song every day while working: 'Wanakiri, Wanabéri.' By this means Spider hoped to fix Death's name in their memory so that it would not be forgotten.

For six months, no other song was heard in that household. It pounded with the pestle crushing the millet, it blew with the fan winnowing the husk from the grain. That song accompanied the jug to draw water at the well, it heard all the stories of the village, and returned home between the high walls of the compound. It went to the fields with the woman in the morning, and kept time with the hoe tending the rows of maize or millet or digging the sweet potato. And in the evening the same song rocked the child and lulled him to sleep.

But the seventh month came, and only one word was left of the song.

In the eighth month there was only a tune.

By the ninth month it was only as dust in dust.

But at last the twelfth month came. There came the last day of the twelfth month, the three hundred and sixty-fifth day of the year and finally the last hour and the last minute of that day.

Then suddenly, there came a knock at the door.

Spider called out, 'Who is there?'

Back came the grim answer: 'It is I, Death. Can you tell me my name?'

'One moment!' cried Spider in panic. 'It is hidden in my granary!' Quickly he ran to his wife. 'That song I told you to sing! Do you remember it? What is Death's name?'

Spider's wife had forgotten, but any answer was better than no answer, so she told him, 'Dindin-Dingouna!'

Spider was greatly relieved, went back to the door where Death was waiting, and replied, 'Dindin-Dingouna!'

'Oh indeed! So you call that my name?' cried Death in fury and triumph, and he snatched up Spider and strode off, carrying him away.

In the yard the wife was weeping bitterly as she realized what her forgetfulness had led to. Her son asked what the matter was, and she told him.

'Wait!' the child cried, and he rushed to a tree, climbed as high as he could, saw Death going away and carrying off his father and cried out, 'Wanakiri! Wanabéri!'

Spider was saved, and Death went away.

Every good son knows there may be debts to pay after the death of his father.

(from *Myths and Legends of Africa* by Margret Carey)

Exercise 5.10

Three narrative extracts follow. Each describes an execution. Consider:

1) The point of view each is seen from.

2) Which aspects are concentrated on in each case.

3) What each passage seems to be telling you, about:
   (i) the people involved,
   (ii) life and death.

Finally draw up a list of useful *Narrative Techniques*, i.e. methods you can use, when writing narrative accounts, to make them more effective and interesting.

(a) Shooting the priest

A small man came out of a side door: he was held up by two policemen, but you could tell that he was doing his best — it was only that his legs were not fully under his control. They paddled him across to the opposite wall; an officer tied a handkerchief round his eyes. Mr. Tench thought: But I know him. Good God, one ought to do something. This was like seeing a neighbour shot.

Of course there was nothing to do. Everything went very quickly like a routine. The officer stepped aside, the rifles went up, and the little man suddenly made jerky movements with his arms. He was trying to say something: what was the phrase they were always supposed to use? That was routine too, but perhaps his mouth was too dry, because nothing came out except a word that sounded like 'Excuse'. The crash of the rifles shook Mr. Tench: they seemed to vibrate inside his own guts: he felt sick and shut his eyes. Then there was a single shot, and opening them again he saw the officer stuffing his gun back into his holster, and the little man was a routine heap beside the wall — something unimportant which had to be cleared away. Two knock-kneed men approached quickly. This was an arena, and the bull was dead, and there was nothing more to wait for any more.

(from *The Power and the Glory* by Graham Greene)

(b) A hanging

The gallows stood in a small yard, separate from the main grounds of the prison, and overgrown with tall prickly weeds. The hangman, a grey-haired convict in the white uniform of the prison, was waiting beside his machine. He greeted us with a servile crouch as we entered. At a word from Francis the two warders, gripping the prisoner more closely than ever, half led, half pushed him to the gallows and helped him clumsily up the ladder. Then the hangman climbed up and fixed the rope round the prisoner's neck.

We stood waiting, five yards away. The warders had formed in a rough circle round the gallows. And then, when the noose was fixed, the prisoner began crying out to his god. It was a high, reiterated cry of 'Ram! Ram! Ram!' not urgent and fearful like a prayer or cry for help, but steady, rhythmical, almost like the tolling of a bell. The hangman, still standing on the gallows, produced a small cotton bag like a flour sack and drew it down over the prisoner's face. But the sound, muffled by the cloth, still persisted, over and over again: 'Ram! Ram! Ram! Ram! Ram!'

The hangman climbed down and stood ready, holding the lever. Minutes seemed to pass. The steady, muffled crying from the prisoner went on and on, 'Ram! Ram! Ram!' never faltering for an instant. The superintendent, his head on his chest, was slowly poking the ground with his stick; perhaps he was counting the cries, allowing the prisoner a fixed number — fifty, perhaps, or a hundred. Everyone had changed colour. The Indians had gone grey like bad coffee, and one or two of the bayonets were wavering. We looked at the lashed, hooded man on the drop, and listened to his cries — each cry another second of life; the same thought was in all our minds: Oh, kill him quickly, get it over, stop that abominable noise!

Suddenly the superintendent made up his mind. Throwing up his head he made a swift motion with his stick. 'Chalo!' he shouted almost fiercely.

There was a clanking noise, and then dead silence. The prisoner had vanished, and the rope was twisting on itself. We went round the gallows to inspect the prisoner's body. He was dangling with his toes pointed straight downwards, very slowly revolving, as dead as a stone.

The superintendent reached out with his stick and poked the bare brown body; it oscillated slightly. 'He's all right', said the superintendent. He backed out from under the gallows, and blew out a deep breath. The moody look had gone out of his face quite suddenly. He glanced at his wrist-watch. 'Eight minutes past eight. Well, that's all for this morning, thank God.'

(from *A Hanging* by George Orwell)

(c)   **The execution of Rubashov**

It seemed to him that they had been walking along this corridor for several minutes already. Still nothing happened. Probably he would hear when the man in uniform took the revolver out of its case. So until then there was time, he was still in safety . . .

A dull blow struck the back of his head. He had long expected it and yet it took him unawares. He felt, wondering, his knees give way and his body whirl round in a half-turn. How theatrical, he thought as he fell, and yet I feel nothing. He lay crumpled up on the ground, with his cheek on the cool flagstones. It got dark, the sea carried him rocking on its nocturnal surface. Memories passed through him, like streaks of mist over the water.

Outside, someone was knocking on the front door, he dreamed that they were coming to arrest him; but in what country was he? . . .

A shapeless figure bent over him, he smelt the fresh leather of the revolver belt; but what insignia did the figure wear on the sleeves and shoulder straps of its uniform — and in whose name did it raise the dark pistol barrel?

A second, smashing blow hit him on the ear. Then all became quiet. There was the sea again with its sounds. A wave slowly lifted him up. It came from afar and travelled sedately, on a shrug of eternity.

(from *Darkness at Noon* by Arthur Koestler)

Write a short passage of about 500 words on one of the following topics:

1) A Day in the Life of . . .

2) Write a short story in ONE of the following styles:
Science Fiction/Horror/Whodunnit/Romantic.

3) The First Time.

4) A report on 'The Match of the Century'.

5) 'I'll never forget . . .'

6) Where were you when the lights went out?

7) . . . so the moral is . . .

Dialogue

(a) **A** You got a cold?

B No — just a bit sniffy cos I'm — I am cold and I'll be all right once I've warmed up. Do I look as though I've got a cold?

A No — I thought you sounded as if you were

B Mm

A Pull your chair up close if you want. Is it?

B Yes. I'll be all right in a minute — it's just that I'm . . .

A What have you got?

B Stupid. I had er about five thousand books to take back . . . and I got all the way through the college to where the car was at the parking meter at the other end and realised I'd left my coat in my locker and I just couldn't

A Mm.

(from an actual conversation recorded in *Investigating English Style* by D Crystal and D Davy)

(b) **Jerry:** Let me kiss your hand, your little, tiny, white hand.

Boyle: Your little, tiny, white hand — are you takin' leave of your senses man? *(Mary breaks away and rushes out.)*

This is nice goin's on in front of her father!

Jerry: Ah, dhry up, for God's sake! *(He follows Mary.)*

Boyle: Chiselurs don't care a damn now about their parents, they're bringin' their fathers' grey hairs down with sorra to the grave, an' laughin' at it. Ah, I suppose it's just the same everywhere — the whole worl's in a state o' chassis!

(from *Juno and the Paycock* by Sean O'Casey)

(c) 'Miss Storey', said Sister, 'you are behaving most foolishly, and I must ask you to leave at once.'

'I won't leave,' I said. 'You'd much better take me straight there, I don't want to be compelled to wander round upsetting the whole of your hospital until I find my baby.'

'Now then, now then,' said Sister, 'this is neither the time nor the place for hysterical talk like that. We must all be grateful that your child is . . .'

'Grateful,' I said. 'I am grateful, I admire your hospital, I admire your work, I am devoted to the National Health Service. Now I want to see my baby.'

(from *The Millstone* by Margaret Drabble)

(d) 'Three hundred degrees centigrade, mind!' said Horrocks. 'It will boil the blood out of you in no time.'

'Eigh?' said Raut, and turned.

'Boil the blood out of you in . . . No, you don't.'

'Let me go!' screamed Raut. 'Let go my arm!'

(from *The Cone* by H G Wells)

Some points to consider

A *Variety* can help. For instance, don't just write '. . .' he *said*. Consider appropriate alternatives, e.g. *asked/replied/called/shouted/ whispered/ muttered.*

B *Examples* can help to liven up a dialogue, e.g. when a character says 'I remember . . .' and goes on to give an interesting anecdote or memory.

C *Conflict* is perhaps even more effective in this respect. In plays some of the most interesting moments come when there is conflict between characters (physical or verbal) — or sometimes even within a person's mind ('Should I, shouldn't I?' as in Hamlet's famous line, 'To be or not to be?')

D Dialogue can be used to *indicate*:

1 *country of origin* (e.g. in passage (b) Ireland: *chiselurs* for *children* and *chassis* for *chaos*)

2 *occupation* (e.g. a soldier might use military terms, a doctor medical terms etc.)

3 *social class* (e.g. in passage (c) the indications are, from the way Miss Storey speaks, that she is middle class: there is no dialect and she speaks in long but coherent articulate sentences).

79

E *Dialect: a warning*. This can be difficult to keep up. Remember that dialect may have a different grammar (e.g. *I be* for 'I am') as well as a different vocabulary (e.g. *thee* for 'you'). If you write in dialect some examiners may wonder whether you can actually write 'correct' English. Sometimes dialect is more effective if used as a *contrast* to standard English.

F Dialogue should be *appropriate* to the *type* of character and the *situation* he is in. One lorry driver is not likely to say to another 'I say, look here, old chap!'

G Dialogue can help make each character a *distinct individual*, for instance if a character is given a particular way of talking or a characteristic catch phrase.

H The way people *actually* talk (see passage (*a*) and also Chapter 1, 'Writing and Talking — are there two English languages?') is not always a good guide — in particular the way they 'um' and 'er' and 'well' and repeat themselves. Don't bore your reader to death. Keep the language appropriate — but keep it moving!

I Unless you are writing a play, remember the *punctuation rules* for dialogue — that is, new speaker, new line.

Exercise 5.12

Write on one of the following:

1) A conversation between two different kinds of people.

2) 'What are you doing here? . . .'

3) A difficult conversation I have taken part in.

Persuasive writing: arguing a case

Well look this isn't an argument!
Yes it is!
No it isn't, it's just contradiction!
No it isn't!
It is!
It is not!
Look you just contradicted me!
I did not!
Oh you did!
No, no, no!
You did just then!
Nonsense!
Oh look, this is futile!
No it isn't!
I came here for a good argument!

No you didn't, you came here for an argument.
Well an argument isn't just contradiction.
It can be!
No it can't. An argument is a connected series of statements intended to establish a proposition.
No it isn't!
Yes it is! It's not just contradiction!
Look, if I argue with you I must take up a contrary position.
Yes, but that's not just saying, 'No it isn't'.
Yes it is!
No it isn't! Argument is an intellectual process. Contradiction is just the automatic gainsaying of any statement the other person makes.
No it isn't.
Yes it is!
Not at all.
Now, look!

(from *Monty Python's Previous Record*)

This passage shows one of the problems of argumentative writing. In everyday life an argument can be simply two people shouting at one another. When presenting an argument in writing, however, more is needed. For instance:

A   A collection of *facts* which, taken together, support your case is obviously useful. So, do some appropriate background research first. (It helps to indicate where the 'facts' came from, to indicate how reliable, up-to-date they are etc.)

B   *Opinions* can also prove useful — but the opinions should be those of relevant *experts*, e.g. if it is a medical question the views of doctors, and particularly of specialists, would be most appropriate. The views of famous figures (film stars, singers, politicians etc.) may have a certain glamour — but are no more reliable on areas they are not expert in than the views of anyone else.

C   *Anticipating* opposing views, by listing them and explaining their weaknesses, may sometimes seem difficult. If you can do it, however, it makes your case much stronger. In a sense it suggests that *you* are an expert, familiar with *all* the arguments.

D   *Variety of wording* helps avoid monotony. Suppose you were writing about marriage. One of the facts your research came up with was that in 1976 in England and Wales there were 356,000 marriages and 146,415 divorces. This indicates to you that many people are now dissatisfied with marriage (though to 'prove' this you would also need to know how many of those who divorced later married again, i.e. were they dissatisfied with marriage or just their current husband/wife?) and that it is no longer stable (more figures, showing how long marriages last, and how this compared with the past, would also be needed to 'prove' anything).

You could word this point in a variety of ways — for example,

- The fact that marriage is no longer the stable institution it once was is now clear from official figures — 146,415 divorces in 1976 alone!

- Official figures on divorce (146,415 in 1976) suggest that marriage is no longer a permanent institution.

- The fact that marriage is no longer seen as permanent is indicated by official figures: there were 146,415 divorces in 1976 alone.

Complex figures can also be simplified. Our figures above could be restated as: for every two marriages in England and Wales there is now one divorce.

You may still find it difficult to put this advice into practice, so let us look at a few examples.

(a) It can be said to its credit that advertising has cultivated appreciation of better living. It has encouraged the desire for a varied and sensible diet. It has introduced appliances and tools which make home and office and factory work less tedious and tiring. It has stimulated our ambition by awakening desires which we can only satisfy be increasing our earning power.

This extract lists points in favour of advertising — but offers no proof. For example, we have to take the writer's word for it that advertising has encouraged sensible diets — he gives no facts or figures to support his claim. This then is a *weak* argument.

(Can you think of any examples to support the points made about advertising — and thus help to produce a stronger argument?)

(b) Now most people take in most of their information from pictures. The washing instructions on your shirt or skirt and the markings on the knobs and levers in your car are symbols not words. And you don't have to read any more to find the right 'loo': an outline figure tells you which door.

This is a *stronger* argument because the main point, that most people take most of their information from pictures, is supported by *three* separate examples. Even so, is the argument conclusive? If pictures are so important why doesn't the writer use some himself?

(c) **TV — renting or buying**

The advantages of renting a television set are that the cost for the first year is less than the outlay would be for buying, and you do not have to pay for repairs or service calls. However, the set never becomes yours, so you cannot sell it, and you have to go on paying rent for as long as you keep the set.

All in all, if you have the money, it is cheaper to buy. Even if you buy on credit, by the end of the third year you will have paid for the set and for the next few years the set will have a resale value, too. Your only expenses would be on repairs.

(from *Which?*)

Here we see a more *balanced* argument. The writer gives some of the advantages of renting, and then some of the advantages of buying, before reaching his conclusion ('it is cheaper to buy'). This weighing up of the arguments gives us more confidence in the writer's conclusion. He seems to be giving an unbiased and objective account, based on the facts. However, even here, some specific figures, showing the costs of renting as against buying a typical TV, would have helped.

As *Which?* magazine does regular tests on consumer goods, like TVs, we can also count their advice as *expert* opinion. So, even though they don't give specific figures we can take it that they know what they are talking about.

(*d*) The 'essay' as traditionally conceived has many disadvantages, especially in the form in which it usually appears in an examination paper. It is very unfair to expect candidates in their predicament as silent prisoners, without access to information sources, notes, dictionaries etc., and with only an hour in which to write, to produce lively, relevant, and intelligently robust comment on generalised topics such as 'The Right to Strike', 'Living in Suburbs', "A House is a Machine for Living in" (*Le Corbusier*).

(from *Notes on the setting and marking of Examinations in English for National Certificates and Diplomas in Business Studies*)

(*e*) Girls are still encouraged to think that their only aim in life is to get married, have children, and then vaguely live happily ever after. There are two things wrong with this life: first, it has become a sentence of solitary confinement with hard labour, leaving the prisoner with no role to play on release; second, society has such a low opinion of it that it doesn't seem worth doing at all.

(from *His and Hers* by Joy Groombridge)

These two passages are interesting because the two writers, although concerned with quite different topics, have both used the same technique. They have both used the same *emotive* word to appeal to the reader's emotions. Passage (*d*) describes candidates as *prisoners*; passage (*e*) describes housewives as *prisoners*. The idea, in both cases, is to produce sympathy for the people described by poetic exaggeration of their plight.

This is permissible in persuasive writing, and is a very powerful technique. But it should be used *as well as*, and not instead of, hard evidence (facts, figures etc.).

(f)   'Well, we have ideas too,' the lieutenant was saying. 'No more money for saying prayers, no more money for building places to say prayers in. We'll give people food instead, teach them to read, give them books. We'll see they don't suffer.'

'But if they want to suffer . . .'

'A man may want to rape a woman. Are we to allow it because he wants to? Suffering is wrong.'

(from *The Power and the Glory* by Graham Greene)

Sometimes it is worth taking an argument to its logical conclusions to see if it is still sound. In this passage the argument of the second speaker is that people should be allowed to do what they want (even if what they want is to suffer). This may seem fair enough. However, this argument can be taken too far, as the first speaker's reply shows. Some things a person may want to do cannot be allowed (e.g. rape). So, allowing something *just* because a person wants to do it, may not be a good argument.

When considering an argument, therefore, it is sometimes worth asking *WHAT IF?* and taking the argument one stage further.

Exercise 5.13

Several extracts follow. For each one, consider the following:

1)   What is the main point the writer is making?

2)   Does he make it at the beginning or end of his writing?

3)   What evidence does he give?
(How many examples and illustrations, what facts or figures? How much is fact and how much is opinion?)

4)   Does he take different points of view into account?
(If so, which?)

5)   Does he use emotive words to argue his case?
(If so, which?)

6)   How varied is the writing? Is it interesting to read?

7)   What kind of reader do you think it is aimed at?
Give reasons for your choice.

8)   Finally — do you think the writer has made out a good case?

(a)   Woman of Africa
      Sweeper
      Smearing floors and walls
      With cow dung and black soil,
      Cook, ayah, the baby tied on your back,
      Vomiting,
      Washer of dishes,
      Planting, weeding, harvesting,
      Store-keeper, builder,

Runner of errands,
Cart, lorry,
Donkey . . .

Woman of Africa
What are you not?

In buibui
Your face is covered
In black cloth
Like a bat's leather wing,
Harem
Private collection
Of tasty flesh

*

In Buganda
They buy you
With two pots of beer,
The Luo trade you
For seven cows
They purchase you
On hire purchase even,
Like bicycles

You are furniture,
Mattress for a man
Your arm
A pillow
For his head!

Woman of Africa
Whatever you call yourself,
Whatever the bush poets
Call you
You are not
A wife!

(from *Song of Ocol* by Okot p'Bitek)

(b)   **The vacuum**

In the last ten years of educational experiment, via unstreaming
and banding, setting in subjects and grouping in houses, we have
practically destroyed the form structure. Last year, my son did not
have one single lesson together with the whole of his form. At
home, he has a gang, and friends he can rely on; at school, no gang
and no friends to rely on. So comes the stage of alienation where a
boy can be punched in the stomach and lie on the ground till he
recovers, while hundreds pass by uncaring. Why should they
care? He is not in their gang; he is not their friend.

In such a gangless unstructured situation, the vacuum grows. As
schoolboys, we loved hot classroom debates, arguing with masters
and testing adult wisdom. Now I find boys will not open their
mouths. Not for fear of the teacher, but for fear of what their
contemporaries will make of any rash statement, afterwards.
One first-former I know admitted that he missed his dead father.

85

Even now, in the sixth, he suffers from taunts of 'Rent-a-Dad, Rent-a-Dad'.

At home, the vacuum grows. The older I get, the more I become aware that my adolescent world-view was built up over many evenings at home, pretending to read a book but really listening to my parents talking to each other. Evenings of what we would now regard as tedium and boredom. Such a world-view had its faults; it was narrow and parochial. But what is sound and narrow can be built on later. At least my parents' world-view was of a piece, graspable.

Now we have the goggle-box. To me, the worst thing about the goggle-box is that it presents a series of vivid, disturbing, disconnected fragments that can never hang together. How can any child, unaided, put together a world-view from a Kojak episode, a nature-film about the Wild Dogs of Africa, and a documentary on Hong-Kong prostitutes? It takes me all my time. The best thing I do for my son is to watch telly with him, exchanging loud and heated commentary while the programmes are in progress (much to the annoyance of my wife).

But what of children who view alone, and see the battered face of a man murdered in Northern Ireland suddenly flashed, without warning, on the screen? Do they despair of ever making a world-view that fits together? Do they despairingly settle for a life of disconnected fragments that are therefore meaningless?

(from *The Vacuum and the Myth* by Robert Westall in *Teenage Reading* ed. Peter Kennerley)

(c) A tribe, a village, later on a nation just came to set up one group of qualities as 'masculine' (those which were most useful in the jobs the men were doing) and another group as 'feminine' (those most appropriate to women's work). For example, we tend to think that women are 'bad at business', 'silly about money', 'no good at arithmetic'. But we belong to that part of the world which put farming down as a man's job, with the trade which developed from it. In Africa, where women were more likely to look after the agriculture, they are still thought to be more businesslike than men, and better at buying and selling.

Indeed, we simply can't say whether any particular kind of quality or aptitude is 'masculine' or 'feminine'. There is no way of telling. Most, if not all, of our behaviour is learned. Future research on the brain may reveal some differences, but meanwhile all we can say with certainty is that a child brought up as though it were of the opposite sex is unable to change back later. Most of us do what we are expected to do, and we are what we are expected to be.

You can see how flimsy this structure of 'manly' and 'womanly' characteristics is if you think again about the 'obvious' physical differences. I said that men on average are taller than women. So they are, but if you look round among the people you know you will almost certainly see that some of the women are taller than some of the men. And we believe that men are stronger than women, and so should do the jobs which involve heavy lifting and carrying. It partly depends, of course, on what the weight is. A woman struggling along the road with a twenty-kilogramme sack of potatoes would probably be offered some help, where the same woman carrying twenty kilogrammes of tired two year old would not. Physical strength is developed according to expectation and training; it is not simply a question of natural ability. In other civilizations, women are thought to be better equipped than men for heavy manual work: in Vietnam, for instance, the dock labourers are women; in Malaya women do the unskilled work in the building trade, such as digging foundations.

As far as intellectual ability and personal aptitudes go, if we must think in terms of 'masculine' and 'feminine' at all, it would be more helpful to imagine a sliding scale with maleness at one end and femaleness at the other and most of us somewhere about the middle.

(from *His and Hers* by Joy Groombridge)

(*d*)

Beyond the original Soviet Union there are the European nations under Soviet power. There are Estonia, Latvia and Lithuania, nations which have actually been incorporated in the Soviet Union against their will. There is Poland, and oppressed Czechoslovakia, whose Government is uniquely contemptible even among Soviet Governments, so panic-stricken that it is even terrified of Aristotle. Timid and guilty tyrants who are traitors to their own nation, fear the most distant echo of truth. There is Bulgaria, which shares with Libya the nervous gangster's habit of assassinating its émigrés. There is Hungary and Rumania, and there is East Germany, with its great wall to keep its citizens in.

That makes a total of nine European nations which have been enslaved by the Soviet Union. Not one of these nine nations would support its Soviet or Communist rulers in a free election. Although some

have been enslaved for over forty years, and all for over thirty, their nationhood and their desire for independence remain. What scorn one must feel for those statesmen who rule them, surviving either on the basis of their own powers of repression or on the power of Soviet tanks.

This tyranny knows no bounds but the world; the claim and the threat of Soviet power is universal. Wherever that power is found there are the same evidences of nations suffering under its violation. We should particularly note how men will risk death to escape life under communism. At this very moment small boats that cannot stand the weather, are putting out from Cuba, as they put out from Vietnam. To a citizen of a Communist regime it is not just the personal threat of prison from which he flees, common though that threat is; his whole nation is in prison.

Beyond that there are nations which have freed themselves from the Soviet

Union, but not from communism. These have ranged from the most unspeakable regimes, like that of Pol Pot — murder by the million — to a regime, Tito's Yugoslavia, which has moved back some way towards liberty. China is still a most repressive regime; China shares our fears of the Soviet Union, but the Chinese regime itself remains an example of repressive Communism.

Many good people wish to forget, to forget Afghanistan, to forget Pol Pot, to forget the Vietnamese or Cuban boat people, to forget Czechoslovakia, to forget the KGB and to forget Stalin. If we wish to survive we cannot afford to forget. It was indeed a wise Government that gave us a May Day holiday of remembrance, knowing that May Day is the day on which the Soviet barons celebrate the achievements of their power and is also the internationally recognised call signal of distress.

(from *The Times*, May Day 1980)

Exercise 5.14

Fact and opinion

These words are often used when describing argumentative or persuasive writing. What do they all mean and can you give an example of each?

fact	rationalise	reasoned
opinion	substantiate	radical
evidence	satirise	reactionary
conjecture	ironic	exaggerated
interpretation	emotive	objective
generalisation	biased	evaluate

Exercise 5.15

Sample topics for essay writing, research or discussion

1) 'Man is actually the weaker sex.' Discuss.

2) In the Soviet Union everyone is supposed to be given a job and everyone is supposed to work. Should the same system be introduced in Britain?

3) Is strict observance of fashion a sign of weakness?

4) 'Marriage is an outdated institution.' Do you agree?

5) The Police: our friends or enemies?

6) 'We have become a nation of spectators.' Discuss.

7) Can hijacking and terrorism ever be justified?

8) The biggest problem facing young people today.

9) 'Government of the rich by the rich for the rich.' Do you think this an apt description of Britain today?

10) The secret of happiness.

11) Is there a Generation Gap?

12) What do you feel gives your life meaning?

Short stories

A check list

As you read a short story ask yourself these questions — they may help you to decide how good the short story is, and *why*:

1 How short is the story actually? Would it have been better longer — or even shorter?

2 Are there any characters in the story who are unnecessary, i.e. would have been better left out because they distract your attention from the central figure?

3   Are there any actions or events in the story which are unnecess-
    ary, i.e. would have been better left out because they distract
    your attention from the main actions/events?

4   Look again at the beginning. How far advanced is the situation
    before the story opens? Is there too much background infor-
    mation given? Could it have been left out/condensed/introduced
    incidentally as the story progressed?

5   Does the story line (plot) follow a common formula? Such a
    formula might be:
    (i)   the eternal triangle (two men, both in love with the same
          woman; or two women, both in love with the same man);
    (ii) a mistaken identity, or a mistake about someone's status
          (e.g. the poor beggar boy turning out to be a rich prince);
    (iii) a love story (e.g. boy meets girl, boy loses girl, boy gets girl
          back);
    (iv) a mystery (e.g. a whodunnit).

6   Look again at the ending. Is there a 'twist' in it? If so, does it
    seem artificial or natural?
    Does a short story need a 'twist' at the end incidentally?

7   Does the story follow Edgar Allen Poe's prescription for a short
    story: i.e., it should work out a single idea; make a single point;
    close with a single 'punch'; convey a single effect; the opening
    paragraph (and even sentence) should strike the keynote – and
    no diversion be allowed?

8   Did you enjoy the story – and if so was it because of, or despite,
    the points considered above?

The short story that follows is set in South Africa.

The waste land

The moment that the bus moved on he knew he was in danger, for by
the lights of it he saw the figures of the young men waiting under the
tree. That was the thing feared by all, to be waited for by the young
men. It was a thing he had talked about, now he was to see it for
himself.

It was too late to run after the bus; it went down the dark street like
an island of safety in a sea of perils. Though he had known of his danger
for only a second, his mouth was already dry, his heart was pounding in
his breast, something inside him was crying out in protest against the
coming event.

His wages were in his purse, he could feel them weighing heavily
against his thigh. This was what they wanted from him. Nothing
counted against that. His wife could be made a widow, his children
made fatherless, nothing counted against that. Mercy was the unknown word.

While he stood there irresolute he heard the young men walking towards him, not only from the side where he had seen them, but from the other also. They did not speak, their intention was unspeakable. The sound of their feet came on the wind to him. The place was well chosen, for behind him was the high wall of the convent, and the barred door that would not open before the man was dead. On the other side of the road was the waste land, full of wire and iron and the bodies of old cars. It was his only hope and he moved towards it; as he did so he knew from the whistle that the young men were there also.

His fear was great and instant, and the smell of it went from his body to his nostrils. At that moment one of them spoke giving directions. So trapped was he that he was filled suddenly with strength and anger, and he ran towards the waste land swinging his heavy stick. In the darkness a form loomed up at him, and he swung the stick at it and heard it give a cry of pain. Then he plunged blindly into the wilderness of wire and iron and the bodies of old cars.

Something caught him by the leg, and he brought his stick crashing down on it, but it was no man, only some knife-edged piece of iron. He was sobbing and out of breath, but he pushed on into the waste, while behind him they pushed on also, knocking against the old iron bodies and kicking against tins and buckets. He fell into some grotesque shape of wire; it was barbed and tore at his clothes and flesh. Then it held him, so that it seemed to him that death must be near, and having no other hope he cried out, 'Help me, help me!' in what should have been a great voice but was gasping and voiceless. He tore at the wire, and it tore at him too, ripping his face and his hands.

Then suddenly he was free. He saw the bus returning and cried out in the great voiceless voice, 'Help me, help me!' Against the light of it he could plainly see the form of one of the young men. Death was near him, and for the moment he was filled with a sense of the injustice of life, that could end thus for one who had always been hardworking and law-abiding. He lifted his heavy stick and brought it down on the head of his pursuer, so that the man crumpled to the ground, moaning and groaning as though the world had been unjust to him also.

Then he turned and started to run again, but ran first into the side of an old lorry that sent him reeling. He lay there for a moment expecting the blow that would end him, but even then his wits came back to him, and he turned over twice and was under the lorry. His very entrails seemed to be coming into his mouth, and his lips could taste sweat and blood. His heart was like a wild thing in his breast, and seemed to lift his whole body each time that it beat. He tried to calm it down, thinking it might be heard, and tried to control the noise of his gasping breath, but he could not do either of these things.

Then suddenly against the dark sky he saw two of the young men. He thought they must hear him; but they themselves were gasping like drowned men, and their speech came in fits and starts . . .

Then some more of the young men came up, gasping and cursing the man who had got away.

'Freddy,' said one, 'your father's got away.'

But there was no reply.

'Where's Freddy?' one asked.

One said, 'Quiet!' Then he called in a loud voice, 'Freddy'.

But still there was no reply.

'Let's go,' he said.

They moved off slowly and carefully, then one of them stopped.
'We are saved,' he said. 'Here is the man.'
He knelt down on the ground and then fell to cursing.
'There's no money here,' he said.
One of them lit a match, and in the small light of it the man under the lorry saw him fall back.
'It's Freddy,' one said, 'He's dead.'
Then the one who had said 'Quiet' spoke again.
'Lift him up,' he said. 'Put him under the lorry.'
The man under the lorry heard them struggling with the body of the dead young man, and he turned once, twice, deeper into his hiding place. The young men lifted the body and swung it under the lorry so that it touched him. Then he heard them moving away, not speaking, slowly and quietly, making an occasional sound against some obstruction in the waste land.

(*A short story* by Alan Paton)

Exercise 5.16

1) Now look back at 'Short stories: a check list' (pp. 88–9) and discuss the effectiveness of this particular example.

2) Complete any *three* of the following:

   (i) 'The young lieutenant lay beside the war correspondent and admired the idyllic calm of the enemy's lines through his fieldglass . . .'

   (ii) 'One confidential evening, not three months ago, Lionel Wallace told me this story of the "Door in the Wall . . ."'

   (iii) 'Three hundred miles and more from Chimborazo, one hundred from the snows of Cotopaxi, in the wildest wastes of Ecuador's Andes, there lies that mysterious mountain valley, cut off from the world of men, the Country of the Blind . . .'

   (iv) 'The man with the scarred face leant over the table and looked at my bundle.
   "Orchids?" he asked . . .'

   (v) 'The lieutenant stood in front of the steel sphere and gnawed a piece of pine splinter. "What do you think of it, Steevens?" he asked . . .'

   (vi) ' "What if I die under it?" the thought recurred again and again as I walked home . . .'

   (vii) 'Until the extraordinary affair at Sidmouth, the peculiar species Haploteuthis ferox was known to science only generically, on the strength of a half-digested tentacle obtained near the Azores, and a decaying body pecked by birds and nibbled by fish, found early in 1896 by Mr Jennings, near Land's End . . .'

   (viii) 'The night was hot and overcast, the sky red-rimmed with the lingering sunset of mid-summer. They sat at the open window, trying to fancy the air was fresher there . . .'

(ix) 'Mr Coombes was sick of life. He walked away from his unhappy home, sick not only of his own existence, but of everybody else's . . .'

(x) 'He sits not a dozen yards away. If I glance over my shoulder I can see him . . .'

Incidentally, the above are all opening lines from *Selected Short Stories* by H G Wells. *After* you have written your versions compare them with his.

Reviews

Reading a review can help you decide whether or not to read a particular book, go to see a particular play or film, or watch a particular TV programme. That's because, generally speaking, they are written by people who have read them or seen them, for the benefit of people who haven't. They try to give a good idea of what the book or film or whatever is like — but without spoiling the story.

Book reviews

(a) These can be very short. Look at these, for instance:

Jackson. *The exam secret*

'It isn't a matter of knowing all about your subject, it's a matter of knowing all about exams.' An interesting and amusing book on examination technique.

Freeman. *How to study effectively*

This small book, produced for the National Extension College, is good for taking you further into studying successfully.

Baker. *A guide to study*

For a little extra, this booklet is intended to give 'general guidelines to study which all students should be aware of.'

Buzan. *Use your head*

A very interesting book, based on BBC television programmes, and giving insight into the whole process of studying effectively. A must for anyone who is really interested in achieving.

Cassie and Constantine. *Student's guide to success*

Apart from thoroughly covering study techniques, this book is also concerned with the student after he or she has left college.

Rowntree. *Learn how to study*

A book for you to work through, answering the questions correctly before you go on to the next section.

As you can see, even a short review can tell you quite a lot. However, it has to leave a lot unsaid and we have to take the writer's word for a lot of things. There just isn't room for more detail or examples. Usually, therefore, a book review will need more detail — and thus be much longer. Have a look at this one, for instance. It appeared in a local newspaper. How much does it tell you about the book? Does it encourage you to want to read it?

(b) Recalling the years of change for all

Compulsive. One word that spells the very essence of a good book. And speaking as one who digests around 60 a year, coming across the sort which causes pans to burn and unwashed dishes to pile up is indeed a rare event.

I have sometimes found this literary quality in a factual book. Never in a novel — until ten years ago when I read a book by Kathleen Conlon. It was her first novel and it was called *Apollo's Summer Look*.

I picked it up, and couldn't put it down again.

Four days ago I repeated this experience when I received a review copy of a book called *A Move in the Game*. First inclination was to relegate it to third place on my current book list, but the author's name — Kathleen Conlon — rang a distant bell of a decade ago and, to put it succinctly, I got stuck in!

For seven hours I was immovable. Colleagues thought I was skiving. Usual routine interruptions took on the proportions of major disasters and, 355 pages later, my list of folk to phone had grown alarmingly.

To describe *A Move in the Game* as eminently readable doesn't really do justice to either the book or its extremely talented author.

The fact that she's a local woman — she lives in Birkdale — is almost irrelevant, except for the fact that Southport is so much richer for her work.

A Move in the Game begins one September day in 1960 when a coach crash wiped out most of the high school sixth form in a small country town.

Linked thereafter were three very different girls, Beatrice, Joanna and Madeleine.

For the next 17 years their lives, and those of their men, formed a complex ever-changing pattern as they pursued careers, or opted out of the rat-race, married, remained uncommitted, had children and love affairs, and ultimately found themselves.

But what they found was not always what they expected, and there lies much of the compulsive fascination of this very skilfully constructed novel, which is a detailed, yet subtle evocation of the years 1960–77, which brought about so many changes in the lives of Kathleen's three characters, and indeed, in all our lives.

One specific sentence for me, forms the crux of the book and it is this: "If I could only go back and stand beside the me of that time, and try to understand how I felt, how I saw things, then I might begin to know what I'm all about."

Overheard conversations, drawing on her own experiences and those of others, plus a remarkable insight, sensitivity and understanding of life and of women, have combined with the author's imagination to produce a book which must become a best-seller.

This novel deals with the trials and triumphs of the three characters whose lives are charted, sometimes dramatically, sometimes humorously, with a great feeling and insight, and it retains, at all times, superb realism.

A former Southport High School girl, who used to work as a 'general dogsbody' at a local hotel, Kathleen Conlon is a true professional.

A Move in the Game is no forgettable romantic novel. It is too realistic, too dramatic and at times too earthy to satisfy a reader who is searching for a happy-ever-after romance.

Nor would I denigrate book or author by recommending it as 'women's reading'. It's a book for everyone, and one which many men would do themselves a favour reading.

A Move in the Game, a Collins hardback, was published on Monday. The lorry drivers' strike will probably cause delays in getting it to our local bookshops.

Keep your eyes open, and find Kathleen Conlon. You may even find yourself.

(from *The Southport Visiter*)

Exercise 5.17

Have *you* ever tried to write a book review? If so, you may have found some problems thinking what to say once you'd told the story. Well, the story *is* important (though if you tell it *all* you'll spoil it for someone who hasn't read it). But there is more to a book than the story. To help you, try filling in a copy of the questionnaire that follows for a book that you have read recently. This should give you a lot more to write about (and think about).

Book Review (Literature)

(where options are given, delete as applicable)

1) *Title of Book*

   Author   Publisher

   Length   First published in

   Type of book   Price

   Novel/play/collected short stories

2) *Subject Matter*

   History/Crime/War/Mystery/Travel/Romance/Sex/Society/Sport/ Politics/Philosophy/Science Fiction/Horror/Other (please state).

   Film and TV Links

   This is/is not a book of a Film/TV series.

   A Film/TV series has/has not been made of this book.

3) *The Story/Plot* (*A Summary*)

   (maximum length one paragraph please)

4) *The Beginning*

   It takes time to 'warm up'/It caught my interest right from the start/It never really got going.

   e.g. . . .

5) *The Ending*

   It was what I expected/It was a surprise.

   i.e. . . .

   Everything was sorted out at the end/I was still left wondering . . .

6) *The Characters*

   I learnt about the main characters through:

   what they thought/what they said/what they did/what others thought about them/what others said about them/what others did to them.

   Relationships develop and change/They remain static.

   e.g. . . .

   Characters are complex and do not fit into easy categories/They are one-dimensional, 'stock' or typical figures.

   e.g. . . .

7) *Themes*

The book dealt with/did not deal with important ideas.
e.g. . . . .

These ideas were stated by the writer himself/by a major character/ were not explicitly stated but were implied or suggested in some way.
e.g. . . . .

8) *Location/Setting/Environment*

Not described/described for its own sake/details described to give a realistic effect of time and place/described to help create an atmosphere/described to show how it affects or is affected by the characters/symbolic.
e.g. . . . .

9) Have you read any other books *by the same author/on a similar topic?*

If so, please state them:

Was this book better/worse/about the same as the others?

10) *Style*

(Your answers to the previous six questions will have given you quite a few examples of the writer's style — for example,

what he chooses to include and to leave out;

what he chooses to describe (or not to describe) about people, places and ideas;

how he starts, finishes and otherwise organises the book;

how obtrusive the writer was (did he keep making comments or did he let the story get on with itself?).

If any characteristics of the writer's style stand out say so and give examples . . .

11) What kind of readers (age/sex/interests) would you recommend this book to?

12) *What you Liked About this Book*

I found this book very entertaining/interesting/amusing/exciting/ thrilling/sad/tragic/enjoyable/absorbing/other (please state).
especially when/for instance when . . .

13) *What you Disliked About this Book*

I found it rather boring/shallow/unimaginative/superficial/predictable/old-fashioned/hard to follow/repulsive/other (please state).

I had difficulty finishing it/couldn't finish it.

What put me off was the language/the subject matter/the story line/ the characters/the ideas.
e.g. . . . .

14) *Final Assessment*

One of the best books I've ever read.

One of the best books of its kind.

A good book.

Average: readable, but nothing special.

Below average — not especially readable.

One of the worst books of its kind.

One of the worst books I've ever read.

Exercise 5.18

That was a questionnaire for a fictional book (novel, short story, etc.). Try making your own questionnaire for a non-fiction book (e.g. on travel, sport, fashion, vehicle maintenance, etc.).

Play reviews

Exercise 5.19

Watching a good play performed on stage, in a good production, is quite a different thing from reading through it in class. I've often found my students surprised to find just how much of a difference there can be. Should you be able to go and see a play, here is a short questionnaire to help you, together with some notes. They should help you notice more about what is going on.

If possible, fill this in *while you are watching the play* — if you become too interested in the story to do this *fill in some sections during the interval.* In any case add comments *as soon as possible afterwards*, e.g. on the coach/train going back if you have travelled far to see a play. The quicker you do the report the more you will remember!

A   **The Play**

Title of play

Writer

Group producing the play

Theatre (or other location)

Was there a good story?

What was the story?

(A very brief summary)

Best part of play
(Why?)

Worst part of play
(Why?)

Were the characters realistic?
(Why/Why not?)

Did the play have something to say?
(Did it have a *point* or a *message*
— if so — *what?*

Or was it just entertainment?)

What was the language of the play?

(modern/old-fashioned? which century?)
(upper-class/middle-class/working-class?)
(BBC English/regional English? which region?)
(natural speech/blank verse/verse?)

(Delete as applicable above)

B The Acting

Audibility (could you hear all the actors?)
(who couldn't you hear — and why?)

Vocal Range (speed, intonation, sound, moods displayed by voice etc.)
(Which actor used his voice to the best advantage? and which actor used his voice to the least advantage? What was the overall standard?)

Best Actor (Who — and Why?)

Worst Actor (Who — and Why?)

Consider: (i) movement and use of gesture; (ii) use of the stage; (iii) interaction between actors (were they just making speeches or were they responding to each other?); (iv) credibility (were they believable in the part they were playing?); (v) interest (did they hold your interest and attention?); (vi) pace (did they rush through their speech and movements too quickly — or drag them out too long — or go at just the right speed?)

Overall standard of acting (considering the points above)

Grouping (How did the actors arrange themselves on stage?)

C The Production

Sketch (i) pictures of the stage, (ii) costumes, (iii) how the actors were positioned in some scenes, (iv) what areas the lights covered, etc.

Type, Number etc.	Reason for use	What was added to or lost from performance as a result
Stage		
Lighting		
Costume		
Make-up		
Scenery		

Audience Response Was the audience response the same as yours — if not, why not?

What did you learn from this production?

How did it compare with other productions seen?

Was the play a good choice (considering the resources available)?

Play reviews: further suggestions

Reviews of plays seen should operate via *evaluation and analysis* rather than just description/narrative; i.e. *why and with what effect?* Consider the following:

A   *Lighting.* Was it used: to indicate the time of day or night; to replace curtains (e.g. ending scenes by blackout); to create atmosphere (e.g. menacing); to focus the audience's attention on certain characters; to provide surprise effects/to change or reflect mood? Did it combine with effects listed below to give an integrated production (e.g. had make-up and lighting been coordinated)?

B   *Sound effects.* Were they used to give an impression of what could not easily be presented on stage (e.g. a battle, traffic etc.); to complement what was being shown on stage; to provide/reflect/change mood and atmosphere (e.g. 'creepy' music)? Were they used in conjunction with e.g. lighting? Were they realistic?

C   *Costume.* Was it used: to indicate social class/occupation/status/character; to build up an impression of realism (e.g. authentic 'period' costume)? Was the costume accurate in every detail – or were selected but significant details chosen (e.g. Shakespearian stage, a turban for a Turk)? How well did costume work overall (e.g. *all* of same period/carefully contrasted styles to reflect differences of class, occupation, character etc.)?

D   *Staging.* Did this: enable the production to flow smoothly; focus attention on, or distract from, the actors; make maximum use of the space available; enable the audience to see or hear particularly well; involve the audience; create atmosphere?

E   *Acting.*

(i)   *Voice.* Was this used: to express feelings (e.g. harsh/tender); to indicate social class or regional location (accent and dialect); to express character (e.g. a deep manly voice or a high effeminate one)? Was there a significant change of voice (as in *My Fair Lady*)?

(ii)   *Body language.* Was this used: to express status (height/unmoving = dominance?); to express feelings (turning back on someone, moving away or vice versa); to emphasise what is being said (e.g. a gesture such as banging on the table); to contradict what is being said (e.g. a wink or inappropriate facial expression)?

F   *Set design.* Was this used: to give an impression of detail realism (exact details); to indicate time and place via a few selected items (audience's imagination to do the rest)? Was it dispensed with altogether to focus attention on characters?

G   *Make-up.* Did it: complement or change the actor's face (e.g. to change age or sex); integrate with lighting and costume; contrast between characters to indicate differences (e.g. was it overdone for a lady of 'easy virtue' but sparingly used for the virtuous heroine)?

Film reviews/previews

Exercise 5.20

The extracts that follow describe two very different types of film. In what ways are they the same as, and in what ways are they different from (i) each other, (ii) from other reviews you have read?

(*a*)   Nile File

A dozen stars, a classic Agatha Christie mystery, an enormous budget — it's the formula that worked superbly as far as EMI was concerned three years ago with *Murder on the Orient Express,* which made more money than any other British picture. The question is can its producers — Lord Brabourne and Richard Goodwin — pull it off again — this time with a different star cast, an even bigger budget of around £4 million, another famous Christie whodunnit, most of it set on a steamer in the exotic reaches of the Nile rather than aboard a snow-bound European train? *Death on the Nile* is directed by John Guillermin of *The Towering Inferno* and the remake of *King Kong,* from a screenplay by Anthony Shaeffer who wrote *Frenzy* for Alfred Hitchcock. Peter Ustinov follows in the footsteps of Finney as the pudgy Belgian sleuth, Hercule Poirot. In this film a wealthy, spoilt heiress is shot through her beautiful skull on her honeymoon while cruising on a steamer, the SS *Karnak.* The other passengers all have the hand of suspicion laid on them in turn as the genuine clues mingle with the red herrings. The motley includes Bette Davis, Angela Lansbury, David Niven, Mia Farrow, Maggie Smith, George Kennedy, Olivia Hussey and Jane Birkin, all playing characters who either have motives, or are not what they seem. Cast and crew spent five sticky weeks on location in the heat of Egypt before retreating to the cool and welcome stages of Pinewood. If nothing else the film will look good — it is being photographed by that Technicolour veteran of the British cinema, Jack Cardiff, who started back in 1937, and the stars are sumptuously dressed in the crêpe de Chine style of the early Thirties by Anthony Powell, who has won an Oscar as a costume designer.

(from a report in *The Sunday Times* by George Perry)

(*b*)   Lonesome Road

Billy was brought up in the city centre of Liverpool, where a typical childhood was enriched by a weekly pilgrimage to Saturday matinee shows at the local picture house. Here Billy would sit spellbound watching his heroes — the Matinee Cowboys.

The years passed, his father ran away leaving his mother to bring him up alone. Re-organisation of the city centre meant they had to move to Kirkby, a new satellite town of Liverpool, where Billy eventually left school only to spend the next two years on the dole.

After two years of boredom he was overcome by a feeling of hopelessness and began to withdraw into memo-

99

ries of his childhood. He relived old fantasies and imagined himself as one of the cowboys, seeing his problems in their terms. The only real thing in his fantasy world was a fast draw game in a city amusement arcade which he always played but never managed to win.

It is through playing this game that Billy meets a lorry driver, a modern day cowboy figure. What the lorry driver tells him leads him to re-examine his situation and to reach the inevitable conclusion for himself and for others like him. At the same time he unconsciously resolves his fantasy.

The story of Billy is told in *Lonesome Road,* a part-documentary part-fiction film, directed by local independent film-maker Chris Malone:

'My original idea was for a short documentary about the sub-culture of Country and Western music against the background of a depressed Merseyside. Inspiration from the Everyman's Western *Kirkby Cowboy* and financial assistance from Merseyside Arts and Sheffield Polytechnic have resulted in what is now a 40-minute colour production in 16 mm.

The problems of choosing the style and format for an independent film are considerable. The style I chose is representative of a television play and therefore has to stand or fall in comparison, although it was shot on a vastly lower budget and with far more limited technical resources.

The main structure of the film is Billy's story but within this framework many other ideas have been woven, broadening its scope and comment. I was not out to give a particular message but ideas just seemed to fall into place. The result, I suppose, is an allegorical tale involving unemployment and the state of Liverpool today using entertaining visual metaphors: the *Lonesome Road* being unemployment itself.

Most of the production work has been completed and the film is currently being edited with an original music score. Filming actually started in the autumn of 1977 with the first of three major shoots; the biggest of these, Billy's shoot, took place in May 1978. The crew consisted mainly of friends from the film department where I was at college or from home in Birkenhead, while the actors were either professionals or talented friends. The leading role was played by Andrew Schofield from Kirkby, a professional actor with plenty of television experience behind him. I am indebted to all the cast as well as the extras and helpers who gave their time and persevered through very difficult situations for little or no financial reward.

Lonesome Road is planned for completion around Christmas this year and will be given a public première in Liverpool.'

(from *Arts Alive, Merseyside,*

Exercise 5.21

1) Most local papers do a brief weekly review of films on in the area. Collect a few of these to read and discuss. (If you go to see any of them, try comparing what you thought of them with what the newspapers said about them.)

2) There are specialist magazines about films (you may find some in your local library). Try to get hold of these and read what they have to say about films. Also try finding some film catalogues (your own library may have some for reference). These often describe and illustrate hundreds of films made over the years.

3) Try producing your own film review questionnaire to help you decide what to look for when watching a film. Next time you go to see a film, try it out.

4) *Television: programme reviews*

The work you have done so far, on reviewing books, plays and films, should make it fairly easy to review individual television programmes so let's go a stage further by looking at different types of programme.

Either individually, or as a member of a group, take a particular type of programme you're interested in:

quizzes, comedy series, sport, domestic serials (Crossroads, Coronation Street. Emmerdale Farm etc.), local affairs, current affairs, detective films, or whatever.

Try to produce a consumer report, comparing the different programmes of that type. If possible try to produce an order of merit, explaining why you believe some programmes are better than others.

Business letters

'Er . . . What was that between Dear Sir and Yours faithfully?'

Confusion is sometimes caused by the fact that there are different rules for typewritten business letters and for handwritten letters. Read the two examples which follow, and see how many differences you can find and list:

101

82, Palace Road,
Loughborough,
Leics. LE8 3ZT.
8th January, 1982.

The Personnel Manager,
Trusty Keg Ales Ltd.,
Mill Lane,
Loughborough,
Leics. LE24 10AB.

Dear Sir,
    I understand that Trusty Keg Ales Ltd.
provides regular guided tours of its brewery,
in order to illustrate the process by which
its 'real ales' are produced, and that these
tours are available to parties made up of
members of local societies or organisations.
    Would it be possible to arrange a visit
by a party of members from our society? About
twenty people would be involved and
we could come any Tuesday or Thursday
evening, preferably in March.
    Please let me know if this would
be convenient.

Yours faithfully,
a. Toper (Miss)
(Secretary, Loughborough
Society for Alcoholic
Research)

(*b*)   Typed (business) letter (model for typing examinations)

TRUSTY KEG ALES LTD

Mill Lane   Loughborough   Leics.   LE24 10AB

Telephone 0509 4464

Our Ref: AG/PT

Your Ref:

12 January 1982

Miss A Toper
Secretary Loughborough Society for Alcoholic Research
82 Palace Road
Loughborough
Leics LE8 3ZT

Dear Miss Toper

Thank you for your letter of January 8 enquiring about a possible visit to our brewery by your members. We do indeed arrange illustrated guided tours and would be happy to welcome you.

Unfortunately our guided tours have become so popular recently that the earliest we could offer you would be the evening of Tuesday, June 1, commencing at 7.30 pm.

It does sometimes happen that a party has to cancel its visit at short notice. In that case we might be able to offer you an earlier date. Do you have a telephone number where we could contact you?

Unless there is an appropriate cancellation in the meantime we look forward to your visit on June 1.

Yours sincerely

A. Griddle
Personnel Manager

Note. The difference between 'Yours sincerely' and 'Yours faithfully' was purely coincidental. The rule remains, whether for typed or hand-written letters:

Dear Sir — Yours faithfully

Dear Mr X — Yours sincerely.

Exercise 5.22

For discussion: business letters

1) Why do you write the name and address of the person you are writing to on the letter as well as the envelope?

2) What is a 'Ref' and why is one given?

3) What advantages have a fully blocked style and open punctuation for typists — and thus for their employers?

4) Has the traditional handwritten layout any advantages?

We are now going to consider two sorts of letter that you might need to write: one for a job application, the other to complain.

Job applications

There are three possible ways in which you might apply for a job:

A You may send a brief letter requesting an application form and then simply fill in the form and return it (with no further letter needed).

B Alternatively you may, when returning the application form, be asked to send an accompanying letter giving more information — for instance, stating why you feel you are suited to the job. In that case, work out what qualities the employer is looking for (what qualifications, what experience, what interests), using the original job advertisement and any further information you have been sent. Then, assuming you have most of the qualities looked for, write a short letter showing this (see 'Making words work harder for you', pp. 106–7).

C If no application form is provided, you will have to include all the relevant information in your letter. It is often easier to write a short covering letter, and then to enclose a separate list of your qualifications and experience. (This list can be photocopied if you are applying for many jobs, leaving you only a different covering letter to write for each new job.) An example follows (* = delete as appropriate).

```
┌─────────────────────────────────────────────────────────────────┐
│                                            Your Address,          │
│                                            (Telephone Number)     │
│                                            Date (in full)         │
│                                                                   │
│  Name and                                                         │
│  Position (of person dealing with applications)                   │
│  Name and                                                         │
│  Address of Firm applied to.                                      │
│                                                                   │
│                                                                   │
│  Dear Mr*/Mrs*/Miss*                                              │
│                                                                   │
│    I should like to apply for the post of              , as       │
│  advertised in the              of              (date).           │
│                                                                   │
│    This job*/This post*/This kind of work*/Your Company*          │
│  particularly interests me because          Also, my             │
│  qualifications and experience (a summary of which I have         │
│  enclosed) seem very relevant.                                    │
│                                                                   │
│    I hope you will be able to offer me an interview, so that I    │
│  can provide any further information you may need.                │
│                                                                   │
│                                            Yours sincerely,       │
│                                            (Signature)            │
└─────────────────────────────────────────────────────────────────┘
```

A summary to accompany the letter could look like this:

Full Name: Qualifications and Experience

(1) *Personal Details:* (i) Full Name, (ii) Age, (iii) Sex, (iv) Marital Status.

(2) *Education:* (i) Full Time — Name and Address of Schools/ Colleges + dates attended + subjects studied, (ii) Part Time — (as above).

(3) *Qualifications:* (indicating dates taken, types of exam, and grades).

   (i) GCEs, CSEs, RSAs, + any other relevant certificates/qualifications.

   (ii) Exams still to be taken.

(4) *Previous Experience:*

   (i) Gained at School/College — where relevant to job.

   (ii) Any jobs done (inc. Holidays or Saturdays) — position, employer, duties.

   (iii) Any relevant special interests.

(5) *Other Material Relevant to Application:*
e.g. interested in nature of work, willingness to train, do day release etc.

(6) *Referees* (Usually two):
Name and Position at School/College/Firm + Address.

(You can also include copies of testimonials where relevant — although employers will usually take more notice of references as these are given in confidence.)

Note. These days competition for jobs can be tough. Hundreds of people may be applying for one job, with maybe only five or six of these being shortlisted and invited for interview. To get an interview your letter of application, or application form, has to stand out from the rest. It needs to be:

• neat and well set out
• carefully worded
• correctly spelt.

To avoid crossings out do a rough draft first, and then a good copy for sending off.

Making words work harder for you

When it's results we're after, we should forget about expressing ourselves, and concentrate on getting through to the other person ... shift the focus from 'What do I want to say?' to *'What results do I want?'*

Exercise
5.23

Read this application that was sent to the personnel manager of a big company:

> I am writing in reply to your advertisement for a secretary/assistant to your Export Manager.
> Your advertisement mentions good typing, and although I can type accurately at 60 wpm, I want a position where I do not have to type very much.
> You also say that a knowledge of French would be an advantage. I do know some French, and would be very glad if the job you are offering would help me improve it.
> I have always wanted to work for a company like yours, because I like all the social contacts you can make in a big organisation. In fact the kind of job I'd really like is a job dealing with people.
> I've already booked up my holidays for this year, and the dates are

The letter goes on like that. The personnel manager said wearily, 'The only thing left out is what she'd like for lunch!'

The writer of the letter did not get on the short list, although the job might have been just right for her. She could have asked about holidays and all the other things at an interview, which she would have been offered if she'd written:

> I can type accurately at 60 wpm. But I am also good at dealing with people, so could bring other things to the job, as well as typing. I already know some French and would work hard at learning more in order to help your Export Manager.

It is saying the same thing — but in a very different way.

(from Getting Through by Godfrey Howard)

Exercise 5.24

Look through the 'Situations Vacant' columns of your local and regional newspapers, or visit your local Jobcentre. (If the week you are looking at doesn't produce anything relevant try back copies in the local library.) Find *two* jobs you are interested in and could realistically apply for. For each write a letter of application. The letters should be different in content and emphasis to the extent that the two jobs are different.

Letters of complaint

HELP! offers some tips on letters of complaint: how to write, who to write to, and how to make your complaint more effective.

Some years ago, as complaints clerk at the world's biggest bookshop, I was astonished to find how diffident the British are when it comes to complaining. Americans whose orders had gone astray phoned from their hotels demanding to know what we were going to do about their missing books. British victims, in contrast, tended to write in apologetic vein: 'Last November I ordered some books for Christmas presents, but I am sorry to say they have not arrived. It may be that they have gone astray in the post, but as it is now July I would appreciate it if you could check to see if they were duly despatched.'

Such a low-key approach is probably as effective as aggressiveness, and illustrates the first of the ten rules for writing letters of complaint.

(1) *Be polite.* Abuse may be satisfying, but is usually counter-productive.

Recipients are likely to respond more seriously to a letter which shows the complainant as a reasonable person — and therefore someone who is the more dangerous. People organising a calm campaign of attrition are more formidable than those who operate by temperamental outbursts.

(2) *Be concise.* Strong points in an argument can be lost or swamped in too much detail. One-page letters are the best letters. A story told in chronological order is the best story.

(3) *Produce evidence.* You should always keep invoices or copies of letters sent to you by a firm or other organisation. Then if promises are not fulfilled, you can write enclosing a photocopy of the document. Keep copies of your own letters too.

(4) *Get the name right.* If you are phoning an organisation and are transferred from one office to another, always ask who you are speaking to. If you are writing, phone beforehand to establish who you should address the letter to. If you simply write to

'The Manager' you may find it impossible, later, to track down the person on whose desk it eventually arrived.

(5) *Take advice*. Epistles along the lines of: 'I want my money back straight away or I'll sue' do not impress professional troubleshooters. It is better to consult with an advice agency in order to establish what your rights are and the best procedure to pursue. The advice centre may help you draft your letter — or might even take up the case themselves.

(6) *Send copies*. An effective and economical way of adding weight to your complaint is to send a copy of your letter to other interested parties. So that if, for example, you are writing to a local shop manager, send a carbon or photocopy to the head office as well. Or, in the case of public utilities, despatch a duplicate to your MP.

(7) *Publicise*. Even more effective, if you are getting nowhere, is to send a copy to your local newspaper, or perhaps one of the consumer columns of a national paper. Or Esther Rantzen? In extreme cases — if the roof of your council flat has fallen in and no one has come round to repair it — write to the paper direct and suggest it might make a news story. Other sorts of direct action — such as setting fire to a defective car outside the garage you bought if from — are tempting but costly.

(8) *Persist*. Many bureaucracies operate on the principle that the machine has more stamina than the individual. Prove they are wrong. If they seem to be procrastinating, badger them to such an extent that it is easier for them to negotiate with you than ignore you.

(9) *Give up*. On the other hand there comes a point when a grievance becomes obsessive, and then it is probably better to forget the whole business. As Christopher Ward sensibly writes in his book *How to Complain*, 'Just walk away from petty disputes and get on with something more useful, more enjoyable.'

(10) *Where credit is due* ... Similarly, when you receive exceptionally good service or value for money, it is only fair you should recognize this by penning the occasional letter of appreciation.

(Bob Smyth in *Radio Times*)

Exercise 5.25

1) **Test on business English and letters**

(i) How many addresses would you put on a personal letter — and whereabouts on the page?

(ii) How many addresses would you put on a formal/business letter?

(iii) If you were handwriting a formal/business letter would you indent the addresses? i.e. _____

_____

_____

(iv) Should you write the date in full on formal letters?

(v) If you start a letter Dear Sir how should you finish it?

(vi) If you start a letter Dear Mr —— how should you finish it?

(vii)   When writing a letter of application for a job what information would you include about yourself?

(1 mark for each point)

(viii) You have written off for a clock radio as a Christmas present. When the clock radio arrives it is the wrong colour and the figures do not light up. What points would you include in a letter of complaint?

(1 mark for each point)

2)   Write a letter in answer to the following advertisement: 'Found, in Baker Street, Newtown, on July 15, a leather purse/wallet* containing a sum of money. Will be returned on satisfactory identification. Write: Smith, 24 Butcher Street, Newtown.'

(*delete as applicable)

3)   Write a letter to the local travel agent, explaining that you and your friend will have to cancel your booking for a week's holiday, and asking for the deposit to be returned.

4)   Write a letter to a former headmaster*/teacher*/tutor* asking if he will agree to act as a referee for you. Tell him about the post you have in mind.   (*delete as applicable)

5)   You are a student who has been asked to leave college by the Principal halfway through the academic year. Write a letter to the Principal appealing against the decision and giving reasons why you should be allowed to continue your course. Supply all the necessary details.

(If you are at school assume you have been asked to leave by the Headmaster. Again, write an appropriate letter to him, appealing against the decision.)

Business reports

'Reports in business do not just happen; they are asked for. Anyone who writes a report does so in reply to an instruction, as part of a routine . . .' etc.

A *routine report* — may be for example:

(i) a standard form to be filled in (Accident Report, Equipment Report, etc.);

(ii) in summary/letter/memorandum form.

A *special report* — which is usually longer, requires investigation or research and is a 'one-off'. The layout may look like this:

```
To:
From:
Date:

    Report on ..........................................
    ..........................................

INTRODUCTION
    a) Terms of Reference
    (who asked for the report, why, and on what area?)

    b) Procedure
    (how you found out the information)

INFORMATION/FINDINGS
    (The Facts — set out via headings, subheadings, numbered points
    etc. Like the whole report this should be easy to 'skim' through — dis-
    regarding points which don't interest. Make this part, although the longest
    part, easy for the reader.)

CONCLUSIONS
    (A summary of the main points)

RECOMMENDATIONS
    (If asked for: what should be done, now the facts are known)

APPENDIX
    (Information, Illustrations etc., too bulky to fit in earlier but to
    which the report refers)

                                                    Signature
```

Organisation of reports

A   Remember the 'Terms of Reference'. Leave out anything not strictly relevant i.e. anything not specifically asked for!

B   When you are clear

(i)   what the facts are,

(ii)   what they, taken as a whole, indicate (without jumping to con- clusions, or omitting inconvenient facts),

(iii)   and what will need to be quoted to make the point.

Then arrange into order: *most important points first*; less important points later.

C   Traditionally reports were written in a formal/informal register — e.g.

It was found that . . .

rather than

We found that . . .

However this can cause problems.

Consider this sentence in a scientific report from Jones and his team, comparing their work with previous work by Smith.

The cats were fed every two hours. Smith found that the cats became angry if they were not. It was found that the aggression of the cats depended on the temperature of the room.

Who made the last discovery, Smith or Jones and his team? Enlightened scientists would now write:

We fed the cats every two hours. Smith found that the cats became angry if they were not and that the aggression of the cats depended on the temperature of the room.

Or:

We fed the cats every two hours. Smith found that the cats became angry if they were not fed. We found that the aggression of the cats depended on the temperature of the room.

Keep your style simple and help others to understand. Don't write 'officialese'!

Exercise

5.26

In each of the following, first discuss/work out what would be realistic Terms of Reference, e.g. who might want to know and why. (See the notes on 'Questionnaires' for the best ways of finding out and analysing information.)

Prepare reports on the following:

1) Leisure facilities for the young people in your area.

2) Study facilities in your college/school.

3) Public transport facilities to and from your college/school.

4) Fashions worn at your college/school.

5) Services provided by a college students' union.

6) Employment opportunities for students in your group:
    (i)   in your immediate area
    (ii) in the region as a whole
    (iii) nationally.

7) Opportunities for part time/holiday work locally.

8) How the average student spends his week.

9) Tobacco/alcohol consumption by the 'average' school/college student.

10) The value of your current school/college course.

Essays

What's your problem?

'I run out of ideas — I can't think what to say'

Try the following — preferably *before* you start writing the essay proper (i.e. in your essay plan).

A   Ask yourself questions about the essay title — e.g.

Who? What? Why? Where? When? How? What if?

B   Especially in descriptive essays think of your *senses* — e.g.

What would be seen? Heard? Smelt? Touched? Tasted?

C   Try a *word association* exercise. Give yourself 30 seconds to jot down the first words that come to mind when you look at significant words in the essay title. This may produce some unexpected ideas or connections.

Try these techniques to assemble as much material as possible on these topics: The local 'Take Away'/Amusement Arcades/Dawn/ Rain/Motorways/A Railway Station/Fog.

D Especially in argumentative/discussion essays look at the title from different points of view — e.g.

Personal, Educational, Cultural, Sexual, Moral, Medical, Environmental, Industrial, Commercial, Economic, Historical, Geographical, Sociological, Scientific, Technical, Psychological, (Super) Natural, Military, Sporting, Political.

(Can you think of any other points of view? Try to suggest another ten.)

To see how this might work, consider this essay:

What have been the effects of television on Britain in the 20th century?

Taking just three of the twenty points of view mentioned in **D** suggested the following ideas to me:

Political. TV is now the main means by which the electorate know politicians (as against public meetings previously). This has changed the style of politics — requiring instant decisions, a good TV manner etc., American experience (when Nixon is said to have lost to Kennedy because his face needed a shave, and it showed) suggests a politician's visual appearance can now win or lose an election. Do politicians need to be TV actors to succeed? (President Reagan *was* an actor!) TV offers great potential for providing information (and does have good news and current affairs programmes, like 'Panorama'). However, viewers are used to dramatic television and so tend to become bored by politics. People then are probably no better informed than before television.

Economic. TV is a major industry and employer in modern Britain (technicians, producers, researchers, scriptwriters, actors, office staff, advertisers, TV factory workers, repair men, rental company and retail staff etc.). Programmes are imported and exported (e.g. 'Daktari' to East Africa) thus affecting the balance of payments. TV advertising is a major stimulus to consumption. Most TV sets are Japanese, Dutch or German — which has an adverse effect on the economy. TV has replaced or slowed the growth of rival media, causing them serious economic problems. Cinema was hit especially hard (many cinemas are now bingo halls).

Sexual. It is always debatable whether TV changes the climate of opinion or just reflects it (for instance, as regards the 'permissive' modern approach to sex). Certainly TV films are more explicit now

113

than say twenty years ago, and 'X' films are regularly screened — but often still censored versions. The nature of TV as 'family entertainment' limits its role as experimenter.*

Despite Selina Scott and Jan Leeming, TV is still male-dominated.

Exercise 5.28

1)   Take three more of the points of view suggested, and see how much more material suggests itself on this essay topic.

2)   Use the technique to gather as many points as possible on these topics: Femininity/Under-age drinking/Masculinity/Emigration/Youth employment.

Another technique for sparking off ideas

Let your mind jump from one thought or association to another. To take advantage of this use a linking out essay plan. This is more flexible and follows the way your mind actually works more closely. For instance, the essay title 'Speed' could conjure up a plan something similar to the illustration on the page opposite.

How to begin an essay

Try to catch the reader's attention.

If you happen to know one, a short story or anecdote with a moral or message relevant to the title is always useful.

Alternative techniques include:

●   An interesting fact . . .

e.g. At the age of ten you reach the age of criminal responsibility and can be arrested, detained for enquiries and charged with a criminal offence.

●   Or figure(s) . . .

A typical load on one 707 freighter flying from Heathrow to Chicago: two poodles, eight plastic bags of eels, a box of radioactive Thorium-X, 5,000 Swiss umbrellas, 500 assorted boxes of goods for a department store, one ton of German cuckoo clocks, six tons of Dutch blankets and £500,000 worth of precious stones.

(from *Airport International* by Brian Moynahan)

●   Or quotation . . .

Marriage is the process by which a man finds out the sort of husband his wife thinks she ought to have had in the first place.

---

*Audience ratings are important: TV gives society what it wants to see, though the BBC probably still feels it has a certain 'educational' role and thus is prepared to experiment — in for instance the presentation of sexual relationships (including sometimes controversial sex education programmes for schools) as well as in other areas like humour (where the BBC has been consistently more enterprising — for instance, with Monty Python-type series).

114

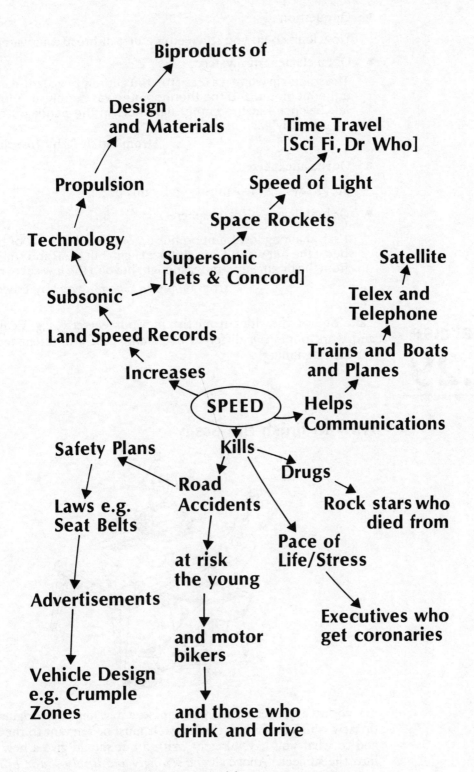

Biproducts of

Design and Materials

Time Travel [Sci Fi, Dr Who]

Propulsion

Speed of Light

Space Rockets

Technology

Supersonic [Jets & Concord]

Satellite

Telex and Telephone

Subsonic

Land Speed Records

Trains and Boats and Planes

Increases

SPEED

Helps Communications

Safety Plans

Kills

Drugs

Laws e.g. Seat Belts

Road Accidents

Rock stars who died from

at risk the young

Pace of Life/Stress

Advertisements

Executives who get coronaries

and motor bikers

Vehicle Design e.g. Crumple Zones

and those who drink and drive

Try this approach with your next essay.

115

- Or question . . .

  How long could you survive on a diet of bread and water?

- Or an element of mystery . . .

  The soldier in white was constructed entirely of gauze, plaster and a thermometer, and the thermometer was merely an adornment left balanced in the empty dark hole in the bandages over his mouth early each morning . . .

  (from *Catch-22* by Joseph Heller)

- Or the unexpected . . .

  Steve says he measures time by tins of peas.

- Or building up an atmosphere . . .

  I sat in a long low bamboo hut on one of a long row of bamboo beds; the hut was full of a diffused light, but clear and still golden, from the bright September sunlight beyond the low eaves outside.

  (from *I am well who are you?* by David Piper)

Exercise 5.29

Take one of the titles from the previous exercise, e.g. Femininity, and work out *seven* different beginnings. Use a different technique for each beginning!

How to finish the essay

Try to leave the reader with a surprise, a new angle, an original point of view which leaves him thinking. (It must be relevant to the subject and to what you have already written but should give a new insight into the subject.) Above all *end strongly and firmly — don't just fade away!* Here are two examples:

(*a*) In 'The Necklace' by Guy de Maupassant a young wife ruins her life to repay the loan she borrowed to replace a friend's necklace she had borrowed and lost. Here is the ending; Mme Forestier, the friend, has finally been told what really happened:

'Mme Forestier, deeply moved, took both her hands:
"Oh, my poor Mathilde! But mine was only paste, not worth more than five hundred francs at most!" '

(*b*) In 'Who Knows?' also by de Maupassant the ending is:

'And I have been here alone for three months, absolutely alone. I have practically no anxieties. I am only afraid of one thing . . . Supposing the second-hand dealer went mad . . . and suppose he was brought to this Home . . . Even prisons are not absolutely safe . . .'

Exercise 5.30

Suggest as many different techniques as you can think of for ending essays. Then, taking any of the essay titles suggested earlier give an example of each type of ending.

Exercise 5.31

What you think: opportunities to state, explain and justify your opinions on a variety of topics

1) What would you do if you heard the world was going to end tomorrow?

2) Love is . . .

3) The kind of government Britain needs now.

4) The home of the future.

5) We often hear people say, 'I know my rights.' What do you think your rights are?

6) Making cities better places to live in.

7) How far is our health in our own hands?

8) The education I should want for my child.

9) Suggest possible uses for the things an average family throws into the dustbin each year.

10) The importance of families.

11) Why I would/would not like to change my sex.

12) 'People just don't understand. If . . .

6

Study skills and research skills

What kind of student are you?

Answer an honest *yes* or *no* to each of these questions:

1) Has your attendance in class been 100% this term (apart from *genuine* illness)?

2) Do you always do work you have been set?

3) Do you always hand it in on time?

4) Do you ever spend 10–20 minutes looking back over your day's notes — and perhaps revising or adding to them — knowing this to be effective revision?

5) Do you spend a few minutes each weekend planning your work for the coming week (to ensure that work and social life complement, not conflict)?

6) Do you keep a clear space for study on a table or desk at home?

7) Do you set aside a regular time for homework/private study each weekday? (This reduces time wasted by indecision and distraction.)

8) Do you use time when you wouldn't be doing much else of use, e.g. travelling to and from college by bus/train, to get school/college work done?

9) When you are asked to read or buy a textbook you haven't got, do you order it well in advance (from the library or bookshop) to make sure you will have it when it is needed?

10) Do you ever test yourself (or work with friends, testing one another)?

11) Do you ever look back over work, making a definite note of any mistakes and deliberately trying to avoid these mistakes in your next piece of work (i.e. do you try to *learn* from your mistakes)?

12) Do you ever ask the teacher, or your friends, if there is a point you don't understand?

13)   Do you ever do reading or research or writing 'around the subject', i.e. on your own initiative, without being told to?

14)   Are you interested in the subjects you are studying?

15)   Will passing the subjects you are studying be useful to you after you leave school/college?

16)   Do you help yourself to remember important points by using aids to memory e.g. mnemonics?
(I can still remember the colour and order of the rainbow
    *R*ed *O*range *Y*ellow *G*reen *B*lue *I*ndigo *V*iolet
from a mnemonic I learned at school
    *R*ichard *o*f *Y*ork *g*ave *b*attle *i*n *v*ain.)

17)   Is your reading speed at least 350 words per minute?
(If not find a book that tells you how to increase your speed and comprehension e.g. *Use Your Head* by Tony Buzan or *Rapid Reading Made Simple* by G K Wainwright).

18)   Do you use different reading techniques depending on what you are reading and why? (e.g. study/slow/rapid/skim and scan: if you don't know what these terms mean, *find out!*).

19)   Do you take notes during lessons, even if no one tells you to?

20)   Do you use your own system of abbreviations, or shorthand, to help you make notes more quickly?

21)   Do you get regular sleep and exercise, so that you are not tired in class and don't miss lessons due to oversleeping?

22)   When you get a low mark do you look carefully to see where you went wrong rather than blaming the teacher, lack of time etc? (again — do you learn from your mistakes?)

23)   Is your handwriting easy to read?
(Be honest — or ask a fellow student to judge.)

24)   Have you made a careful study of your school/college and local libraries to see what materials they have:
    (i)   on subjects you are studying,
    (ii) on topics you are interested in outside of school or college (e.g. sport, fashion etc.)?

25)   Do you know the details of the examinations in your different subjects (e.g. how many papers, how long each is, what format the questions are)?

To calculate how *good* a student you are add up the number of honest *yes* answers and multiply that by four to give you a percentage. The higher the percentage the better a student you should be.

But don't stop here. Where you had a *no* answer do something about it. Then test yourself again in a week's time to see how much your score has improved. Keep on doing this until you have reached at least a genuine 80%. By that time you should also find that you are doing more work and getting higher marks. In short you will have become a *better student*.

Exercise
6.2

Now live up to your good intentions by finding out the answers to these questions about the school/college — and help yourself to be a better student:

1) Have you done a thorough survey of the *school/college library*? (see 'Using libraries, pp. 125–6).

2) Is there a *school/college bookshop*?

3) Is there a *school/college shop*? If so, *does it stock stationery* (pens, pencils, paper, folders etc.)?

4) If the answer to either of the above is *no*, where is *the nearest bookshop* — and where is *the nearest shop which sells stationery*?

5) Is there a *school/college careers officer*?
What is his/her name?
Where is he/she available,
and when?
Is there a *school/college careers office*?
Where is it situated?

6) Is there an examination office, where you can go to check about exam entries and results?
If so, where is it?

7) Is there *a noticeboard* in school/college *for your course*?
If so, where is it?

8) Is there a *student union office*?
If so, list the services it offers.

9) Are there any *evening classes* which you could join to assist your studies (i.e. relevant to subjects you are already taking) to follow up or enlarge your own interests?
If so, give details.

10) Are there any *student counsellors*?
(Staff available to help students with problems — be they personal, financial or academic.)
If so, who are they; where can they be contacted — and when?

11) List *the staff who teach you*. For each indicate which staff-room they are in should you need to contact them urgently.

12) Are there any *student societies* concerned with:
   (i) the subjects you are studying
   (ii) your own interests and hobbies?
If so, give details.

13) Are there any *photocopying facilities* for students? If so, where and how much does each copy cost?

Reading skills

When I test the accuracy and speed of reading of students in my classes I usually find that I can read *two or three times faster* than them, yet still get as many correct answers. This is true even with, for instance, BEC National Diploma Classes. Now obviously this has advantages for me: I can choose either to do more work in the same time as them – or to do the same work and have more spare time. Either way I benefit. Yet they – and you – could be in the same position if you improve your reading skills. If you are interested, read on.

An efficient reader can do 500 words a minute – what is your reading speed?

How to read faster

(especially with everyday material, which is not especially difficult, and doesn't need special study).

A Widen your eye span to take in more words: don't 'fixate' on every word – take in small groups of words at a time. (To help you do this – don't move your head as you read – and don't follow individual words with your finger or pencil.)

B Don't regress, i.e. don't go back over material you have just read – keep on reading. (To help you do this put a card over the material you have already read and move it along accordingly.)

121

C Don't subvocalise i.e. don't mouth the words silently to yourself — your eyes and brain can move faster than your lips.

D Try to achieve a *reading rhythm.*

E Just try *aiming to read faster* (will power?).

How to read better

A Ask yourself *why* you are reading. (This will help you decide what to look for and remember, and what you don't need to worry about.)

B Choose a place it is easy to *concentrate* in. (Otherwise you will be distracted — and you can't do two things at once.)

C (A long-term aim) *Read widely* to increase your knowledge and vocabulary. (Practice makes perfect — and the more you know the less chance there is of being confused by difficult new words, which slow you down.)

D Try to *anticipate* and *read critically.* Don't just accept what you read. Ask yourself questions about it e.g., Can he prove this? Whose side is the writer on? Is he being serious here? etc., etc. (Be an *active* not a passive reader.)

E Look for the *main points* (often the writer will help you by using **HEADINGS**, subheadings, BLOCK CAPITALS, underlining words or putting them in *italics*). Sometimes the main point will be expressed in the first sentence of a paragraph and the rest of the paragraph will simply illustrate this main point.

F *Test your comprehension* as you read. Mentally summarise what you have read. Ask and answer questions. (If you are working with a friend test each other — or discuss what you have read.)

G *Relate what you read to your own experience and draw your own conclusions.* Make the material your own — something you know and have views on — a part of you. Again — be an *active reader.*

H Above all *read for enjoyment.* Choose books on topics you are interested in. One topic may lead to another. The more you read, the more reading will become a pleasant habit and the less effort it will seem or be. Are you really enjoying that TV programme — if so, fine, keep watching. But if not, pick up a book. Remember: libraries are free; there is no book licence; and books come in colour as well as black and white.

Reading: the 'gears' or speeds

Some reading is more difficult; some is more important. Adjust your reading speed and technique accordingly. Experts identify four main 'gears'.

First: Study Reading (up to 150 words per minute)

For difficult and/or important material: Skim read/Re-read/Note/Revise/Think about and Make connections.

Second: Slow Reading (150–300 w.p.m.)

For quite difficult material or to ensure 100% *comprehension*. This is how most students read if they haven't improved their reading skills: for them it is 'normal' speed.

Third: Rapid Reading (300–800 w.p.m.)

For average or easy material where the aim is to have a general, but not necessarily 100% understanding.

Using the techniques suggested in 'How to Read Faster'.

Top: Skimming/Scanning (800 + w.p.m.)

Reading rapidly for general impression or to locate specific information.

This technique pays particular regard to *cues*, e.g. headings, first sentences etc. (See B above.)

An example would be looking through a telephone directory to find a name — you only read what is absolutely necessary.

Where can I find out more about reading?

You have just read a very brief summary. You will find more information, examples, tests and explanations in books like these, which your local or college library may well have:

Read Better, Read Faster by M and B De Leeuw (Pelican)
Use Your Head by Tony Buzan (BBC)
Rapid Reading Made Simple by G R Wainwright (W H Allen)
Teaching Faster Reading by E Fry (Cambridge)

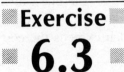

Exercise 6.3

1) Follow-up work

    (i) Look back through the advice on reading and draw up a checklist of techniques you have not used so far. Each time you come to a new piece of reading (e.g. a textbook in another subject, or a novel or short story read for pleasure) try to use some of the appropriate techniques from your checklist. When you find yourself using a technique regularly, cross it off the checklist. That will leave only those techniques you seldom or never use. In friendly competition with a friend see who can reduce their checklist the more quickly.

(ii) Keep a daily log of all materials you have read — including books, magazines, letters, newspapers, handouts from your teachers etc. By each entry put down which 'gear' you read it in. At the end of the week discuss your findings with fellow students.

2) Selecting and reading the right information

First, you will need a good selection of world-wide travel brochures, e.g. Kuoni, Wings, Thomas Cook, from local travel agents.

You are working in a travel agent's and receive a letter asking for details of holidays to fit the following requirements:

- for three adults — two to share a double room, one to have a single room.
- in Kenya, East Africa
- for two weeks
- between 20 July and 20 August
- preferably costing no more than £700 per person all inclusive
- the itinerary to include — some time in Mombasa/on the coast
  — some time on safari in one or more Game Parks
- some guarantee that if the company collapses, money already paid will be returned.

Look through the assorted travel brochures to find all information on holidays in East Africa, and

(i) List holidays which cover the points required or come near — indicating any problems in terms of the original requirements.

(ii) Write to the customer, on behalf of the Travel Agent, advising him of the possible holidays he should consider and suggesting which seems to be the best value.

(If there is no such holiday giving all the points required, please indicate:

- the nearest other holiday in this price range, i.e. the one which has *most* of the stated requirements;
- the holiday with all the points required which exceeds the cost limit by the *smallest* amount.)

(*Note.* This exercise involves: selective reading, comprehension, summary, note-taking and business letter practice.)

Using libraries

Exercise 6.4

Investigate a library (or libraries) using the questionnaire below. You will need one questionnaire for each library.

1) *Library surveyed*: College/Local/Main/Specialist (delete as applicable).

2) *Layout of the Library.* On a separate sheet draw a plan of the library, indicating, via a key, what each section is used for.

3) How many books can you take out of the library and for how long?

How many books have you out at the moment?

Had you used this library before today?

4) List the subjects you are studying. For each subject:
    (i) give the subject's library classification code;
    (ii) mark the location of books for that subject on the plan you have drawn;
    (iii) indicate approximately how many books on that subject are available.

    Subject   Library Code   Number of Books

5) Besides books which of the following facilities are here? newspapers/magazines/records/cassettes/films/newspaper cuttings/ photocopying/other* (delete as applicable).

6) Is the library computerised?
If so, in what ways is it different from a traditional library?

Why do some library tickets now look like this?

Metropolitan Borough of Sefton
Libraries & Arts Services

D 120 025 85X XB

Mr Michael Baber
16 Scarisbrick St S/P
Date of issue   4.6.80

*These vary, e.g. Manchester City Library keeps reading lists for most AEB and JMB A-Level Literature set texts.

7) Is information available on:
  (i) Higher Education (Universities, Polytechnics, Colleges).
  (ii) Careers?
If *yes*, indicate on the plan where this is available.
Is this information in the form of: books/leaflets/prospectuses/films/cassettes/other? (delete as applicable).

8) Is this library usually:
  (i) too hot/too cold/just right;
  (ii) quiet/noisy;
  (iii) empty/half full/full;
  (iv) a very good/adequate/poor place to study in? (delete as applicable).

9) Do the librarians seem helpful?

10) List your interests/hobbies:
For each:
  (i) name any relevant magazines the library has;
  (ii) indicate the number of books on the subject;
  (iii) indicate any other relevant material.

Interest	*Magazines*	*Books*	*Other Material*

11) Briefly explain the Inter-Library Loan System.
(If you don't know what it is — find out.)

12) (i) Has the library sufficient tables and chairs?
  (ii) How many people could sit and work in the library at any one time?
  (iii) How many librarians are normally on duty?
  (iv) What are the opening times of this library?

13) Give *three* bad points about this library.

14) Give *three* good points about this library.

Surveys and questionnaires

*"Forgive me, but it's been a long
time since my opinion's been asked."*

These days surveys are big business. Companies carry out surveys to check if new products will sell. Newspapers carry out surveys to check what people think about social and political issues — and, of course, who will win the next General Election. The demand for surveys is such that some organisations have been set up just to carry out surveys (Gallup, Marplan, MORI etc.), whilst major companies have their own survey departments. The BBC, for instance, has its own Audience Research Department, which employs 800 inter-viewers, carrying out several thousand interviews a day throughout the United Kingdom. In addition, the BBC has Listener and Viewer Panels of ordinary people who are sent questionnaires every week: the Listeners Panel alone consists of 3 000 people, carefully chosen. Over the years much has been learnt about what makes a good survey, and you can benefit from this.

Here is a quick guide to surveys and questionnaires:

A What do you want to know — and who will have that information?

B Ask only the people who will have that information. (This may mean only certain age groups, occupations, or people living in certain areas etc. Check this carefully.)

C Asking everyone who has the information usually takes too much time — so ask a *representative sample* (e.g. 1 in 20, 1 in a 100, 1 in a 1000 of that kind of person).

D People don't usually mind answering a few questions — but they are more likely to if they are asked politely, told why you are asking the questions, and assured that their replies will be treated confidentially.

E Even so they may not have all day to stand and answer questions, so try to keep the number of questions reasonably small (no more than ten, for instance).

F Choose your questions carefully. Keep them:
  - short
  - easy to understand, and
  - easy to give an accurate answer to.

Avoid any question that could be ambiguous, misleading, difficult to remember or to remember the answer to, embarrassing, vague, over-technical etc.

G As you will need to record the answers as they are given (for non-postal surveys, anyway) prepare
  - questions it is easy to record answers to. (The answers to multiple choice questions are easy to tick off, and relatively easy to analyse afterwards — e.g.

Do you think xyz is:

not important	LHT //	(7)
fairly important	LHT ////	(9)
important	LHT LHT ///	(13)
very important	LHT /	(6)

Open questions mean you have to write down everything the person says, which gets tiring — and the answers are more difficult to analyse quickly.
  - question forms which are easy to use, and have, for instance, plenty of space to tick off answers.

H When you have all your answers, tot them up, and then present them in easy to follow form. If there are a lot of figures involved, presenting them in the form of tables, graphs, charts, pictograms etc., can help. So too can generalisations — for instance, 'The vast majority believed . . . , whilst only a few . . .'

I Draw appropriate conclusions from your results. For instance you could say, 'The fact that so many people declared . . . would suggest . . .'

J Remember that a well-conducted survey will usually give a pretty accurate picture — but cannot guarantee 100% accuracy. There are different reasons for this:

- People may make honest mistakes. A BBC survey found that 5% of housewives interviewed were mistaken about what TV channel they had been watching a couple of minutes earlier — probably because they were thinking in terms of *programmes*, not TV channels.
- People may forget, or misunderstand.
- They may be afraid to give an honest answer or embarrassed to.
- They may even just change their minds.
- The representative sample may not have been as 'representative' as it was supposed to be etc.

This is why it is so important to prepare your survey carefully in the first place, and then, when considering the results, to concentrate on the overall picture (which should be fairly accurate) rather than on exact percentages (which probably will not be so accurate). To give an example, opinion polls just before the 1979 General Election all got the right overall picture (the Conservatives would win) but couldn't give the precise figures (there was an average error of 1.7% as regards the gap between Labour and Conservative — and this was a smaller error than usual).

Exercise 6.5

1) If you were preparing a survey on the following, what kind of people would you ask, and what would be a reasonable representative sample:

    (i)   under-age drinking locally;

    (ii)   under-age drinking nationally;

    (iii) local amateur football (from a player's point of view);

    (iv) local amateur football (from a spectator's point of view);

    (v)   perfumes preferred by young women in your area;

    (vi) purchase of perfumes locally;

    (vii) how important local employers think it is for job applicants to have 'good English';

    (viii) what local employers think 'good English' is?

2) Surveys can tell you all sorts of interesting (and uninteresting), useful (and useless) things. Did you know, for instance, that on one evening in February 1980, 3.7 million people stayed up until 3 o'clock in the morning to watch ice-skating on television (to see Robin Cousins win a gold medal for Britain in the Winter Olympics). That's just one of the thousands of figures the BBC surveys come up with every year.

Think of *five* things you would like to know, which a survey could help you find out.

3) Choose *one* topic you would like to know more about. The prepare, carry out, and present the results of a suitable survey. *Als* — keep a list of any problems that you found in preparing, carryin out, or presenting the results of this survey — together with details o how you tried to deal with these problems.

4) This is a major project which will take up quite a lot of time You would probably need at least a month, and preferably a term, o even a whole year, to get a full picture and will need the whole clas working together. Only start if you feel it is practicable.

Prepare a report on 'Job Prospects for Young People' in your area To get a full picture you will need to do surveys of, for instance school and college leavers, local employers, Jobcentres, career officers, situations vacant columns, and so on. The longer you carr out the survey for, the better an idea you will gain of the best time of the year to apply for jobs. For maximum usefulness you will nee to survey not just how many jobs are available, but also how thos that are available are gained. What is the relative importance of quali fications, experience, 'knowing someone', application forms, inter views etc? See the section on 'interviews' (p. 17) in Chapter 2 for a idea of the type of factors that can affect people's chances of gettin a job. As so many things need surveying you will probably need a bi of 'division of labour' — with different students tackling differen areas.

When you've finished the results should be of use to you — giving you an idea of your own job prospects. You might also find tha local newspapers, local radio or even television might be interested i the results. They might even be able to help you by running some parts of the survey for you, or offering suggestions (if you ask nicely! Who knows — if the report is really good they might even conside offering you a job!

*"She always checks up on her facts —
where's the entertainment value in that?"*

Projects

A project usually involves investigating or researching a topic. To help get you started try using a checklist like this:

PROJECT CHECKLIST

Topic

Possible Sources of Information:

     Books   **Magazines/Articles**

     TV/Radio Programmes   **Visits/Interviews**

     Experiments/Observation   **Personal Experience**

Now check off your progress with each of the above, using symbols like these:

Key   * = I have now ordered/arranged this.

        √ = I have now read/completed/carried out this.

Useful Illustrations/Diagrams/Statistics

This topic looks like being too big: I now need to cut out

and concentrate on

(e.g. a shorter period of time/a smaller area/fewer people/ just one aspect or point of view etc.)

                OR

This topic wasn't really big enough. I need to add

The Most Interesting Points are:

The Best Title for the Project will now be:

Exercise 6.6

Careers project

Choose a career you are interested in. Using a separate answer shee[t] you have *50 minutes,* using any source of information (a book, [a] pamphlet, a person, a newspaper etc.) reasonably accessible with[in] the school or college, to

(i) answer the questions below, and (ii) describe exactly how yo[u] went about finding the information.

Career _____

1) What is the preferred age for starting this career?

2) What qualifications are
   (i) necessary,
   (ii) desirable?

3) What would your starting salary be? And what would you[r] maximum salary be?

4) How is promotion gained? (e.g. do you need additional qual[i]fications or training?)

5) Which of the following would be available? (delete if n[ot] available): sports and/or athletics facilities/a social club/paid holiday[s] of ( ) weeks per annum/canteen facilities/luncheon vouchers/trave[l] expenses/removal expenses/a pension fund/a sick pay scheme.

6) What will the working environment be like? (delete if n[ot] applicable): clean/dirty/noisy/quiet/smelly/hot/cold/pleasant/damp[/] dry/modern/old/crowded/comfortable.

7) Is there such a job available locally? If so, how far away, an[d] how long will it take to travel to work, and how much will that trave[l] cost?

8) If you moved to another part of the country would such a jo[b] be likely to be available there too?

9) Have you seen such a job advertised recently? If so, where an[d] when?

10) What sources of information have you found about the job s[o] far?

11) Would there be opportunities for further training whil[e] working?

12) Would you be: mostly working alone/working with others[/] working as part of a team/dealing with people/handling customers['] property/working with mixed ages/handling confidential material[/] working with the opposite sex/doing a monotonous job/be workin[g] in one place/be travelling a lot/using machinery/be using offic[e] equipment?

Getting information: from people

There are various ways of gathering information from people:

- Letters seeking information

  Use Standard Business Letter layout. The key words here are: *Brevity, Clarity* and *Courtesy.*

- Telephone enquiries

  Use Standard Telephone Technique (Why are you ringing?; paper and pen handy; customary greeting, and thanks for assistance at end; be clear; don't rush.) (A name, or extension number can speed up the process — so check who you have been talking to in case you need to ring again.)

- Observation and visits

  (i) If going to a factory/business organisation make a formal request by letter to the personnel manager well in advance (otherwise as appropriate).

  (ii) Go prepared — with a notebook, schedule, and/or portable cassette (convenient at the time — but more work later).

  (iii) Be systematic; check; be unobtrusive (people behave differently if they know they are being observed).

  (iv) Courtesy — check if it is permissible to photograph/sketch/question employees.

- Interviews

  (i) *Formal* — part of a series — each interviewee is asked the same questions — for subsequent statistical analysis.

  (ii) *Depth* — as much as possible from one person — some prepared questions — some in response to replies — taping makes it easier if the interviewee agrees.

  (iii) *Informal* — where isolated information on a specific topic is needed — face to face or on the phone.

People are not surprised to be interviewed these days — but in-depth or specialist interviews still require prior consultation and a written request. What is the interview intended to achieve? Be clear and have a schedule or questions prepared in advance. Be polite (interviewees' time and information is their own and given at *their* discretion) — and thank the interviewee at the end.

Gathering information: from books, magazines, newspapers etc.

- See the sections on 'Using libraries' and 'Reading skills' earlier in this chapter, and on 'Taking notes' in Chapter 7.

- The main thing is: be organised! You'll probably have a lot of information and material. Don't let it overwhelm you.

  Look back to the 'Project checklist', on p. 131. Something like this should help organise your search for material, and help you check your progress. Perhaps more of a problem is what to do with material once you've got it. Hence . . .

- Some suggestions:

  (i) Photocopies save time — but not money.

  (ii) Keep a note of where material comes from (the title and author, anyway) in case you forget it, lose it, or have to return it (a library book, for instance).

  (iii) Write your material on to loose leaf sheets of paper or loose cards.* When you finally come to put the material in order you can then shuffle these sheets into different orders, until you find the one that's best.†

  (iv) A pair of scissors and a pack of Blu-Tack, Platstick etc., can be very useful if you change your mind about the order of items. You can cut a piece off one sheet and stick it on another should you want a different order. (That's what I did when writing the script for this book.)

  (v) Sometimes you'll find you've chosen a topic that's too big. Reduce the topic by concentrating on one aspect of it, or one geographical location, or one limited period of time. The more manageable the topic the more manageable the material should be.

  (vi) Don't be afraid to edit. You don't need to give all the examples you have collected, perhaps — just use the best ones. If some material is wordy, or dull, or over-technical you can summarise it, or reword it.

Presenting information

- See the section in Chapter 5 on 'Business reports' (pp. 109–12).

- Basically, the information, however much there is, should be easy to follow. So *signpost* your progress (especially where the alternative would be a mass of facts and figures) by charts, graphs, pictograms, tables, photographs, diagrams, sketches etc. (as appropriate). *Don't* use illustrations just to fill out your project, or make it look pretty. *Do* use illustrations where they help the reader understand what you are writing about.

*If you are preparing a rough draft before copying up the final version.

†Alternatively, simply writing a one-sentence summary, plus title and page reference, can save you writing material out in full.

- Don't just copy chunks out of books or magazines — anyone can do that. You can copy parts out if: (i) you keep them short, (ii) you add a little note saying where the extracts came from (this being known as 'acknowledging your sources'), and (iii) you couldn't have summed the point up better yourself.

- Even if you have gained most of your information from other people, or other books, *try to reach your own conclusions.* Make up your own mind about what you have found out. This doesn't need to be strikingly original (though a new angle may catch the reader's interest more easily) — but it should at least be what *you think, in your own words.*

Exercise

6.7

Topics for discussion/enquiry/project work

1) Food: One man's meat or another man's poison.

2) Holidays: Around the world in 60 minutes.

3) Science fiction: A brief star-trek.

4) Assumptions — about you, about me, about what we see.

5) Emigration: Living in Britain today — why bother?, what are the alternatives?

6) Hobbies: Old and new — for leisure, for profit.

7) Survival: Common ways of dying — how to avoid them and stay alive.

8) Reading — living with it and without it.

9) Bargains — what to buy, where and when.

10) The weaker sex — men or women?

11) A life of crime — is honesty the best policy?

12) Keep Britain colourful — or would we be better off in an all-white Britain?

13) Unions rule OK. True or false? For better or worse?

14) It's in the stars. Astrology for fun — or a guide to life?

15) Your ideal man/woman. Computer dating — an investigation.

16) Chips with everything — silicon, that is — what they will do to me and for me.

17) Fashion — who makes it, who breaks it?

18) Till death us do part — marriages the world has known.

19) Entertainment — some weirder forms.

20) Happiness — sought/bought/caught/taught?

7 Comprehension, summary and taking notes

There are too many words I can't understand

Here you have several alternatives:

A *Read widely throughout your course* — not just books, but magazines and newspapers — not just fiction but non-fiction too. The more you read, the more words you will come across, and in different contexts. If you take the trouble to look up new words in your dictionary and to make a note of new words (including those in other subjects you are studying), this will help increase your vocabulary. It's common sense — the more words you know, the lower the chance of coming across words you don't know. Try setting yourself a target — to learn and use 12 or 20 new words a week (more if you can). Just twelve new words a week (and you would try to learn more than that if you were learning a *foreign* language) — will give you more than *400* new words over an academic year. Friendly competition with a friend or group of friends can help here.

B *Deduction!* Do you know what *samphire* is? Don't worry if you don't; I didn't know either until a few months ago. But let's suppose you came across the word samphire in a passage on wild plants you can eat, and the actual context was this:

The first time I was offered a whole dish of wild vegetables I was frankly scared. The plant was marsh samphire, a skinny little succulent that grows abundantly on saltings. It lay on my plate like a mound of shiny green pipecleaners . . .

(from *Food for Free* by Richard Mabey)

After reading this you should not only be able to tell me what samphire is, but also where it grows, what colour it is, what it looks like, and whether you can eat it. Not all words, of course, will have quite such a helpful context, but many new words can be worked out with a bit of thought.

C *Ignore*! Not all words are equally important. When you send a telegram you usually miss out a lot of words — but the telegram can still be understood. If the words you don't know are not especially important you can, in emergency, simply pass over them. Let us take that word samphire as an example again. Suppose that the first time you met it was in this extract from Shakespeare's play *King Lear*:

Half way down [the cliff]
Hangs one that gathers samphire, dreadful trade!
Methinks he seems no bigger than his head
The fishermen that walk upon the beach
Appear like mice.

In fact, even here, we get some clues as to what samphire is (the fact that men gather it from the sides of cliffs). But even if we still don't know exactly what it is this doesn't really matter. In this play the samphire is just an incidental descriptive detail and does not have any effect on the main characters or the action of the play. As such it can, if necessary, be ignored. (This, incidentally, contrasts with the previous passage from *Food for Free*! There, the subject of the passage was edible wild plants — and so samphire was, in a sense, a major character, and not to be ignored.)

'I can't follow the argument: what's the writer trying to say?'

"Stop telling callers to take a seat. We've lost 27 chairs this week"

Try looking for *cues*. These are words (or other aspects of the passage, such as underlining, BLOCK CAPITALS etc.) which give you a clue, or act as a signal:

● to tell you *what order* events happened in — e.g.

First/First of all/At first/In the beginning
Before that/Earlier/Previously
At the same time/Meanwhile/Simultaneously
Then/Next/Secondly/Afterwards
Finally/At last/Eventually etc.

- to tell you what are *main points* and what are examples or illustrations of these points:
  - (i) Often the first few lines of a paragraph contain the main point, and the rest of the paragraph just gives further information in the form of examples or illustrations emphasising the original point.

    Sometimes examples are signalled by phrases like

    such as/for instance/for example.

    The opening lines and the closing lines of a passage are particularly likely to contain main points.

  - (ii) **HEADLINES**, <u>underlining</u>, BLOCK CAPITALS etc. are all ways of drawing your attention to main points. Never forget the importance of the *title* of the passage you're reading.
- to tell you the writer is *changing his point of view* and looking at *the opposite side of the argument*. Words like

  However/On the other hand/Despite this/But

  particularly coming at the start of a new paragraph, usually signal a change of direction in the argument.
- to indicate *cause and effect*: that one thing has caused something else to happen. Words to look for here are

  as a result/therefore/thus/consequently/because/since

Exercise 7.1

To check if you follow this, read the passage 'Why go to Polytechnic'.

Why go to Polytechnic?

Why do some students go to polytechnics while others go to other institutions of post-school education? If a student is going to study an HND course or any other non-degree course then the answer will generally be that that particular polytechnic is providing the best course available. However, many students who study for a degree, including myself, only came to a polytechnic because they failed to obtain a place in a university and indeed in my case, not only did I come to polytechnic as a second choice, I am studying for a course that I originally did not want to study.

Such an attitude is unfortunate but it is true to say that many if not the majority of students studying for a degree at a poly are at a poly for the same reason. Polytechnics are regarded by many, including careers masters, as second-class universities and yet there are many advantages in studying at a poly.

Firstly, polys have a far wider level of education to offer.

Secondly, if a student is studying for a degree then that course will probably have been validated by the Council for National Academic Awards (CNAA), a body which is far more prepared to innovate compared with Universities who validate their own degrees.

Thirdly, courses at polytechnics tend to be more vocational than university courses and for many people this is of crucial importance.

Fourthly, poly courses tend to be 'student' centred compared with universities which tend to place far greater emphasis on the course than the student that takes it.

There are, however, very serious problems relating to polytechnic education. Most important is that polys have since their foundation suffered from cash problems. Library facilities, for instance, are in most cases not only overcrowded but also lack all but the most basic facilities. Many polytechnics are multisite institutions and the concept of a corporate institutional identity does not exist.

In London, Thames Poly has a site in West London, a site in South East London and a Teacher Training site in Kent with over 20 miles between them.

In the earlier part of this article I compared poly education with university education. The reason for this is that the majority of those who read this will be trying to decide which college to study at. However such a comparison is incongruous. The roles of polys and universities within the education system are different.

Why were the polys created? They were founded because of Harold Wilson's idea that Britain was in need of the 'White Hot Seat of the Technological Revolution' and were seen as institutions that could provide the 'white hot technocrats' who would run this revolution and the courses would give training for Britain's future engineers, accountants, surveyors etc. This did mean that the nature of post school education would have to change. Universities were seen as giving 'an education for life' with specific vocational training given in only a few specialist subjects such as medicine. Polytechnics were to be financed by Local Education Authorities, to ensure that these institutions would keep to this vocational ethos. Polys are also supposed to be sympathetic towards the needs and aspirations of the local community.

(from *Focus* by R B Taylor)

Now answer these questions on it.

1) What do you think is the main point of the passage, and what clues suggest this?

2) After saying (in the second paragraph) 'Polytechnics are regarded by many, including careers masters, as second-class universities', what one word signals that the writer is now going to take a different point of view?

3) After spending the third, fourth, fifth and sixth paragraphs describing the advantages of polytechnics what one word, early in the seventh paragraph, signals that the writer is now going to look at the opposite side of things (i.e. the problems of polytechnics)?

4) The third, fourth, fifth and sixth paragraphs each deal with a separate advantage of polytechnics. How (apart from giving each point a separate paragraph) does the writer signal that a fresh point is being made in each case?

5) Look at paragraphs seven and eight. The writer makes two specific points about polytechnics and gives a specific example of each point. What are the specific points, and what are the examples?

6) What example of 'cause and effect' occurs in the final paragraph? What word links the cause and the effect?

7) Can you find a parallel example of 'cause and effect', using the same linking word, in the last paragraph?

8) To make a new point. Sometimes a writer will indicate that he is 100% sure about something, for example by using absolute terms like

always, never/will, will not/must, must not etc.

However, life isn't always so straightforward. Often the most that a writer can say is that most of the time something is true. If he can't be 100% sure, he will tend to use words and phrases like

usually, generally, most of the time, in most cases, as a rule, in general.

And if he's even less sure he may have to use words like

probably, possibly, perhaps, may, might, sometimes etc.

Now, look back through the passage and find any words or phrases that signal that what the writer is saying isn't 100% true (not because he's lying but because what he's writing about isn't straightforward — he realises that there may be exceptions to what he's saying).

'The sentences confuse me. They're so long and complicated'

Take a look at this sentence — all 95 words of it:

In the event of loss or damage to this product caused by burglary, theft, or accidental means within 3 (three) years from the date of delivery, or in the event of any fault occurring in the product resulting in the malfunctioning thereof within the same period the manufacturer or the company's accredited retailer from whom the product was purchased will replace such product if it has been lost, repair it if it has been damaged or rectify such faults as have occurred therein, in every case free of charge subject to the undermentioned conditions.

All those words crammed up together do look a bit overpowering. (Incidentally, if you're one of those students who tends to use commas instead of full stops let this be a warning. Full stops give the reader chance to catch his breath (physically and mentally) and follow what you're saying.)

Don't panic. Try the flow chart approach. You should end up with something like the illustration shown opposite.

If you've used flow charts before, this should be fairly easy to follow. If you haven't, there's always a first time.

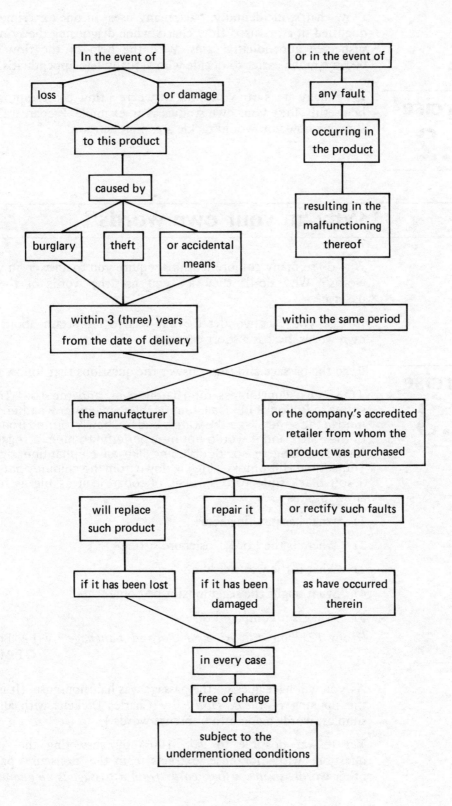

In the event of

loss   or damage

to this product

caused by

burglary   theft   or accidental means

within 3 (three) years from the date of delivery

or in the event of

any fault

occurring in the product

resulting in the malfunctioning thereof

within the same period

the manufacturer

or the company's accredited retailer from whom the product was purchased

will replace such product

repair it

or rectify such faults

if it has been lost

if it has been damaged

as have occurred therein

in every case

free of charge

subject to the undermentioned conditions

141

Flow charts, incidentally, have many uses. In one experiment newly qualified doctors used flow charts when diagnosing the symptoms in suspected appendicitis cases. With the help of the flow charts it became much easier to decide who actually had appendicitis.

Exercise 7.2

How many areas can you think of where a flow chart approach could be useful? Take your own studies as an example. Prepare a flow chart showing how you would tackle a comprehension!

Why 'in your own words'?

Why do so many comprehensions require you to answer 'in your own words'? Why don't they let you use the words of the original passage?

In case you ever wondered what was so important about 'in your own words' here is a short exercise.

Exercise 7.3

Read the passage and then answer the questions that follow:

'LONDON. Pugglemess term lately over, and the Lord Tinslebore sitting in Rinlonks Inn Hall. Immucable November weather. As much mud in the streets, as if the waters had but newly formed from the face of the earth, and it would not be wonderful to meet a seggumpalot, forty feet long or so, doddlebing like an elephantine zig pod up Thursdrible Hill. Smoke gingling down from the chimney pots, making a soft black siffle with sprokes of tooze in it as big as full-grown snowsprokes . . .'

1) What has just finished?

2) Where is the Lord Tinslebore sitting?

3) What is the weather like?

4) What might the seggumpalot be doing?

5) What is it compared to?

(from *Teaching English as a Second Language* by J A Bright and G P McGregor)

As you will have guessed the passage was half nonsense. (It is, in fact, the opening of *Bleak House* by Charles Dickens with all but the simplest words made into nonsense words.)

Yet it was possible to gain 100% by answering the 'nonsense' questions with 'nonsense' extracts from the 'nonsense' passage. In other words, *simply using words from a passage is no guarantee that you understand them.* This is a pity as it means that, to avoid this, some comprehensions become a sort of paraphrase or translation exercise — which is only a part of comprehension (understanding). But how otherwise can your comprehension be checked?

What can comprehensions test?

Let us start by listing possible *skills* or *knowledge* a comprehension may be trying to test:

- *Selective reading* (searching quickly for particular pieces of information, e.g. a name in a telephone directory or a time on a railway timetable).

- *Deduction of meaning from context* (working out the meaning of words you don't know from clues in the other words around them).

- *Existing vocabulary* (knowing what a word means, even without clues from the context).

- *Summary* (ability to select main or important points and discard examples, repetition, 'padding' etc.).

- *Evaluation* (giving an opinion about what is written, e.g. agreeing or disagreeing with it).

- *Analysis* (being able to see what is fact and what is opinion, what is important and what is not, what the writer's attitude is etc.).

- *Inference* (seeing what the passage is suggesting or implying, even if the point is not stated directly or explicitly).

- *Technique of writing (organisation of information)* (analysing whether the passage works by listing events in the order they happened in, by comparing and contrasting, by showing cause and effect, by classifying material into different types, by literal description or imaginative comparison etc.).

- *Information transfer* (can you transfer information from one form to another, e.g. from a graph or chart to continuous writing, from a magazine article to notes, from a phone message to a memo etc.).

- *Overall understanding* (all the above, as necessary).

143

Evaluating a comprehension

A lot of students seem to do comprehensions without realising why (except that one or more will 'come up in the exam'). Yet comprehensions, as I have suggested, are set to test certain skills and it helps to be aware of this. Not all comprehensions are good tests, but even with these it usually helps to know what they are *trying* to test.

Exercise 7.4

Look at the following comprehension test.

First of all, read it and answer the questions, as you would in an exam.

Then, look back at it, and ask yourself how well or how badly this particular test actually revealed your understanding of the passage. In particular look back at the previous section ('What can comprehensions test?') and check how many skills the comprehension was trying to test. Consider too whether the questions set were a fair test. Would they have been better worded another way, or left out altogether? Can you think of questions that *should* have been asked but weren't?

In conclusion — was this a fair comprehension exercise?

The future of television

(1) Television is enjoyed because it is convenient, varied, responsive to the audience and apparently inexpensive to watch (although its costs are hidden: most people spend more on television in a year, in licence fees, electricity and rental, than they do on books and films combined). It is resented by its critics because they say it is ephemeral, that it frequently panders to the lowest common denominator of popular tastes, and that it creates a uniformity of cultural experience. The sense of personal discovery that is in the other arts does not exist for television viewers.

(2) But whatever its critics may say, television in this country has always been an excellent barometer of social change; it moves with the times more responsively than any other popular medium, including, frequently, the Press.

(3) This is because there are two major influences on the sort of programmes we watch, and although they are quite different in kind, they frequently work together to change programme policy. They are, firstly, the degree of technical sophistication available to the programme makers and set-manufacturers, and, secondly, the needs, attitude and response of the audience.

(4) In the area of technology there is virtually no limit to the changes that are possible. Anything that can be conceived is theoretically feasible, and in some instances could be manufactured today if the need existed. There is presently a pocket-sized television receiver, for instance, so how long before the wrist-watch television, or the finger-ring television?

(5) It is even possible that television could be transmitted direct to lightweight headsets, with electronic stimulation of the aural and visual nerves,

so that the broadcast is enjoyed (if that is the word) by seeing inside your brain rather than by looking at a television set with your eyes. This is an awe-inspiring and quite frightening proposition. Imagine the consequences of there being direct access to the minds of the population, if television were controlled by a demagogue.

(6) A less sinister prospect is the fact that there is no upward limit to the size television screens could reach. A screen could be made as big as the wall of a room . . .

(7) The second great influence on television — audience response — will play no less of a role in the future. Today we have ratings, measured in millions of viewers, but one day there may be a more subtle way of gauging what viewers actually wish to see.

(8) The BBC Open Door series has done much pioneering work with 'access' television allowing minority groups to present their ideas or aims, free from editorial control. But 'access' can be achieved in another way, by direct audience response to television shows.

(9) Since December 1977, a new television   station — QUBE,   in Columbus, Ohio — has provided its cable-set subscribers with a computerized keyboard, through which viewers can respond directly to what they see. During certain programmes they can raise an objection, ask for a repetition of an unclear point, show approval or disapproval etc., thus making television accessible to a certain degree. However, those who have seen this in trial operation have remarked on the banality of the result, with the programme effectively reduced to the most crushingly simple-minded levels.

(10) Experiments have also been made to assess the capacity for commercial exploitation: viewers could order goods they saw advertised, simply by pressing a button. Imagine this if it became a world wide phenomenon, and soap powder, holidays, and deodorants, could be ordered through the television set. Would anyone ever go shopping again? What sort of controls would be needed on the advertised goods? What would it do for freedom of choice, for individuality, for specialist or minority needs?

(from *Radio Times* 1978)

Answer all questions *in your own words*, unless otherwise stated.

1) According to the first paragraph what criticisms are made of TV? (4 marks)

2) Choose any *four* of the following and suggest a word or short phrase which could replace each in the passage.

    (i)   *ephemeral*   (paragraph 1)

    (ii) *panders*   (paragraph 1)

    (iii) *feasible*   (paragraph 4)

    (iv) *demagogue*   (paragraph 5)

    (v)   *subtle*   (paragraph 7)

    (vi) *banality*   (paragraph 9)

    (vii) *phenomenon* (paragraph 10)   (4 marks)

3) Explain any *two* of the following phrases, in the sense that they are used in the passage.

    (i)   *the lowest common denominator*   (paragraph 1)

    (ii) *a uniformity of cultural experience*   (paragraph 1)

    (iii) *electronic stimulation of the aural and visual nerves*
                                                 (paragraph 5)

    (iv) *pioneering work with 'access' television*   (paragraph 8)

                                                            (2 marks)

4) In no more than 60 words summarise the technological changes possible in television.   (10 marks)

5) What possible disadvantages of direct viewer response have already been noted?   (2 marks)

6) Direct view response is open to commercial exploitation. What possible consequences could this have? (i.e. what questions might this raise?)   (5 marks)

7) Give *ten* reasons to show why the author seems to approve of television. Here you may quote from the passage.   (5 marks)

DIY comprehension

Now that you have had a brief introduction as to why comprehensions are set — here is a chance to make one yourself. A passage is provided. Work out 8-10 questions which you feel are a *full* and *fair* test of overall understanding. Then exchange questions with another student; he tries to answer your questions, you try to answer his. Afterwards discuss how similar or different your questions were, and what this suggests. Is working out a good comprehension easy?

(a) **Romance: the female fantasy**

The hero of romance knows how to treat women. Flowers, little gifts, love letters, maybe poems to her eyes and hair, candlelit meals on moonlit terraces and muted strings. Nothing hasty, physical. Some heavy breathing. Searing lips pressed against the thin stuff of her bodice. Endearments muttered into her luxuriant hair. 'Little things mean a lot.' Her favourite chocolates, his pet names for her, remembering her birthday, anniversaries, silly games. And then the foolish things that remind him of her, her perfume, her scarf, her frilly underthings and absurd lace hankies, kittens in her lap. Mystery, magic, champagne, ceremony, tenderness, excitement, adoration, reverence — women never have enough of it. Most men know nothing about this female fantasy world because they are not exposed to this kind of literature and the commerce of romanticism. The kind of man who studies this kind of behaviour and becomes a ladies' man whether for lust or love or cupidity is generally feared and disliked by other men as a gigolo or even a queer. Male beauticians and hairdressers study the foibles of their customers and deliberately flirt with them, paying them compliments that they thirst for, hinting that they deserve better than the squalid domestic destiny that they bear.

If *Sweethearts* and the other publications of the same kind with their hallucinated love imagery are American, it is unfortunately true that they find a wide distribution in England. There are also trash weeklies called *Mirabelle, Valentine, Romeo* and, biggest of all, *Jackie* selling upwards of a million copies a week to girls between ten and sixteen years of age, which set forth the British ideals of romance. The girls are leggier and trendier, with tiny skirts, wild hair and sooty eyes. The men are wickedly handsome on the lines of the Regency Buck, more or less dapper and cool, given to gazing granite-jawed into the glimmering eyes of melting females. The extraordinary aspect is the prominence given to fetish objects. Romance appears to hinge on records, books, knick-knacks, and, in one case which appears to the detached observer to be almost surreal, a park bench. Kate and Harry are sweethearts. They sit on a bench in the park and exchange dialogue thus:

'Oh, Kate, I love you more than anything on earth.'

'And I love you more than anything in the whole universe, darling.'

The bench becomes enormously important in their relationship and when the council decides to move it Kate dashes to Harry's office in the Town Hall with a demand that they sit in, on it. Harry does so until his boss, the borough surveyor, tells him he'll lose his job if he holds out any longer. He gives in, leaving Kate to defend her bench alone. She takes it as an indication of the shallowness of his love for her. But one of the people involved in the moving of the bench, obviously a lover because of his granite jaw and Byronic hair, takes his place beside her. 'We'll save this bench for you, for the past and all lovers to come.' The last frame shows our heroine peering dewily at him through tear-dimmed eyes, her baby pouting lips a hair's breadth from his rugged prognathous contours. 'But you'll lose your job for nothing. Do ... do you really think we can beat them,' says her balloon. 'I know we can beat them,' his balloon rejoins. 'People can do anything if they try hard enough and love well enough. Let's try ...' The end, to say the least.

(from *The Female Eunuch* by Germaine Greer)

Some more passages follow for you to prepare questions on (*Down to the Sea, What is a Housewife? Different customs* and *Life and Death*).

(*b*) **Down to the sea . . .**

Students and researchers at Portsmouth Polytechnic are trying to untangle the country's knottiest problem.

It is Sargassum Muticum, a Japanese seaweed that threatens to choke harbours and disrupt fishing along the south coast. Portsmouth

147

biologists and engineers have designed and launched their own boat to fight the menace.

The boat, Toriki, has cutting and trawling equipment which can clear 500 pounds of the world's fastest growing seaweed in a 30-second drag.

The £100,000 project is just one of the ways in which polytechnics are answering the call of the sea.

At North East London Polytechnic the underwater technology unit is busy making life safer for the diver working in the murky depths of the North Sea.

Current research, backed by a £21,000 Science Research Council grant, is looking at medical care for commercial divers, underwater work in zero visibility and diver communications.

But they are also looking ahead to the day when North Sea oil runs out and the platforms have to be demolished. Said lecturer David Baume: "We're examining new and developing applications of underwater technology, such as fish farming and ocean thermal energy conversion. We have to look to the future."

Two Bristol Polytechnic lecturers and a student, on the other hand, are using one of the great sailing vessels of the past to create work for unemployed youngsters.

They are trustees of a charity employing the boys to refit the SV *Pascual Flores,* a two-masted schooner featured in the television series The Onedin Line.

The aim is not only to provide jobs, but to help the youngsters improve their social skills, said Bristol Polytechnic lecturer Dave Brockington.

Polytechnic courses are also gaining an international reputation in the maritime field.

Recently City of London Polytechnic lecturers travelled to Bombay to stage a ten-day residential course for Indian shipping managers. The course was based on the maritime transport day release classes held at the polytechnic.

And at Liverpool Polytechnic a multi-disciplinary team have been working to make sure that ships pass safely in and out of congested ports. Their port information system, based on the Post Office's Prestel equipment, could in the long term provide special warnings of tidal surges, navigation alerts and hazardous goods listings to shipboard terminals.

Work on the system, intended to sort out the jumble of radio, telex and telephone messages, has already resulted in the award of a Master of Philosophy degree to one of the team, electronics specialist, Mark Bradshaw.

Students at Liverpool Polytechnic have also emerged top in recent merchant navy examinations. Engineer officer David Spence from Thingwall, Wirral, received the Nevins award for highest marks in the marine engineer first class certificate examinations, and the Griffiths award went to chief officer Andrew Baker from Bebington, Wirral for coming first in the master's certificate examination.

(from *Focus* Autumn 1979)

(c)   What is a housewife?

No precise figures are available for the number of women who are housewives, but a British survey found that 85 per cent of all women aged between sixteen and sixty-four in a random sample of over 7,000 women were housewives — they carried the responsibility for running the household in which they lived.

While nine out of ten women who were not employed were housewives, so were seven out of ten of those with a job outside the home. Housework is clearly the major occupational role of women today. Employment does not itself alter the status (or reduce the work) of being a housewife.

With the virtual disappearance of the 'underclass' of private domestic servants, housewife and houseworker roles have merged. The average housewife spends between 3,000 and 4,000 hours a year on housework. Housewives in the urban British sample studied by the author in 1971 reported an average of 77 hours weekly housework. The amount of time housework takes shows no tendency to decrease with the increasing availability of domestic appliances, or with the expansion of women's opportunities outside the home. A comparison of data available from different countries over the last four decades (shown in the table below) demonstrates a remarkable consistency in housework hours.

The social trivialization of housework (and of women) is in part responsible for the tendency to underestimate or ignore the amount of time women spend doing it. But other features of the housewife role also conspire to conceal it. Housework differs from most other work in three significant ways: it is private, it is self-defined and its outlines are blurred by its integration in a whole complex of domestic, family-based roles which define the situation of women as well as the situation of the housewife. Housework is an activity performed by housewives within their own homes. The home is the workplace, and its boundaries are also the boundaries of family life.

A Comparison of Data on Housework Hours.

Study	Date	Average Weekly Hours of of Housework
1. Rural Studies		
United States	1929	62
United States	1929	64
United States	1956	61
France	1959	67
2. Urban Studies		
United States	1929	51
United States	1945	
Small city		78
Large City		81
France	1948	82
Britain	1950	70
Britain	1951	72
France	1958	67
Britain	1971	77

In modern society, the family and the home are private places, refuges from an increasingly impersonal public world. There are no laws which oblige the housewife to make the home a safe place for her family, although, by contrast, industrial employers

149

are subject to a mass of controls. There are regulations governing the safety of domestic appliances, but the housewife as the manager of the domestic environment is not bound to see that their safety is maintained (or indeed, to buy them in the first place). Accidents are now the prime cause of death for people under forty-five in most Western countries, and domestic accidents make up the bulk of all accidents. What people do in their own homes is their affair. Physical violence or dangerous neglect subject the lives of six children in every thousand to the risk of mortality.

The physical isolation of housework — each housewife in her own home — ensures that it is totally self-defined. There are no public rules dictating what the housewife should do, or how and when she should do it. Beyond basic specifications — the provision of meals, the laundering of clothes, the care of the interior of the home — the housewife, in theory at least, defines the job as she likes. Meals can be cooked or cold; clothes can be washed when they have been worn for a few hours or a few weeks; the home can be cleaned once a month or twice a day. Who is to establish the rules, who is to set the limits of normality, if it is not the housewife herself?

Housewives belong to no trade unions; they have no professional associations to define criteria of performance, establish standards of excellence, and develop sanctions for those whose performance is inadequate or inefficient in some way. No single organization exists to defend their interests and represent them on issues and in areas which affect the performance of their role. These facts confirm the diagnosis of self-definition in housework behaviour.

(from *Housewife* by Ann Oakley)

(*d*)   **Different customs**

Cultures differ one from another in the use of non-verbal communication. Differences are found in the kinds of signals used and in the meanings given to body movements, eye contact and even the distance apart between people. Comparisons can be drawn between cultures in the non-verbal expression of emotions and in greeting behaviour. A British person covers up his distress with the well-known stiff upper lip, but a Japanese person has been taught to hide his sadness beneath a contradictory smile. Touching forms a part of greeting in many societies. A Latin kisses a lady's hand. Eskimos butt each other on the shoulders. Malayans rub noses. Yet other cultures avoid bodily contact. The Chinese bow. So do Indians, at the same time placing the hands, palms together, in front of the body.

The meaning of non-verbal signals varies with the culture. An Arab learns to stand close to another person in conversation. Amongst Americans, standing close to one another signals intimacy to the other person and to observers. The American chooses a distance that feels comfortable to him when in conversation with another. When two Arabs are in conversation with each other and when two Americans share a conversation,

150

therefore, observers note that Arabs stand closer together than do Americans.

But if two individuals from each culture meet, a confusion of non-verbal signals follows. The American male, unused to close proximity to another man, steps backwards in an attempt to establish a comfortable distance. The Arab, feeling disconcerted by the widening chasm between himself and his conversation partner, moves forward. Both men want to stand at a normal distance from each other, but normality is set by social convention. Each person had learned a different convention for standing in conversation with other persons. To American eyes, two Arabs talking together appear conspiratorial — as signalled by their close proximity. To Arabian eyes, the standoffishness of the American is revealed all too clearly by his insistence on 'keeping at a distance'.

Misinterpretations of other people's conventions are legion. Italian youths frequently hold hands. Greeks stare at strangers. Does the English tourist see the innocent friendship expressed in holding hands? Does he feel the interest of the Greek or does he regard the looks as threats? We cannot help but observe the non-verbal customs with prejudiced eyes. We fail to pick up the meanings of another culture's signals. We misinterpret signals and erroneously draw conclusions about the character of the people. We imply that Arabs must be 'shady' and 'sly' because they are always conspiring. Latin women always 'lead a man on' in the way they flash their eyes. Conspiracy and romantic liaisons are no more common in these cultures than in one's own. But the signals are used differently and are misunderstood by the visitor. In this sense it is more difficult to interact with someone from a different culture. The interaction does not 'feel right', and, consequently, both participants feel anxious and unable to cope.

(from *Communicating Effectively* by Beryl Williams)

(e) **Life and death**

The Trauma Ward (a special unit for the emergency treatment of serious injury) at Cook County Hospital is filled with gunshot, knifing and assault victims — a gruesome collection of injuries which suggests a front-line army first-aid post rather than a public hospital in one of America's largest cities . . .

The impression it gives of a place under siege is not entirely inappropriate. The third largest public hospital in America, with a total of 1,400 beds, Cook County Hospital lies a few minutes' drive from the centre of Chicago, a symbolic dividing-line between the elegant skyscrapers and Picasso sculpture of downtown and the housing projects and timber-framed back-to-backs of the city's South Side Ghetto — an area where supermarket windows are bricked-up and men while away the morning hours on the sidewalk, nursing bottles of cheap wine.

The handbook for Cook County Hospital notes that the hospital is located among (the greatest concentration of medical facilities in the world) a complex which includes no fewer than eight separate hospitals and medical institutes. The irony is that, in a country without a national health service, Cook County Hospital is the only *public* hospital, not simply in the complex, but in the area of Greater Chicago, serving a population of some five-and-a-half million people, 'without regard to social, economic and ethnic differences'.

Its patients are the working — or unemployed — poor; black, latino and a minority of whites; those on the lowest rung of the income ladder, outsiders in a system where health insurance for a family of four can cost 1,800 dollars a year (and contain a clause excluding heart-patients) and the hospital bill for child-delivery can be as much as 4,000 dollars.

Like its patients, Cook County Hospital, too, is caught in a vicious inflationary spiral, battling against closure in the face of rising costs and diminishing subsidies from federal welfare payments and local authority funds.

The tragedy is that the South Side of Chicago, from where most of the hospital's patients come, is precisely the sort of area which most needs a large and fully-equipped hospital. The over-crowding, crime and compounded social problems of the South Side is a recipe for ill-health . . . and a panoply of ailments which are the by-product of neglect, poor nutrition, drug abuse and alcoholism . . .

In an emergency the staff work with the alacrity of Grand Prix motor-mechanics. A man stabbed in the back by his girl-friend with a six-inch hunting knife, is bustled into the ward with a retinue of armed police and medics, stripped, resuscitated, plugged with intra-venous lines, large-bore catheters and a breathing-tube, and packed off to the operating theatre — the knife still in his back — inside 12 minutes. He lives. 'We like to feel', says one intern, 'that if a patient makes it to the emergency-room alive they should leave the hospital the same way. It doesn't happen all the time, but we save a helluva lot more than we lose.'

Cook's reputation is not confined to the medical community. When 37-year-old Roeshell Powell was stabbed in the stomach on the way to visit his mother, he had the presence of mind to specify that he be brought to Cook for treatment. 'I got a bunch of hospitals right near me, but this is the only one I ever come. You get good doctors and the nurses treat you right.' Mr. Powell raises a smile which is heroically cheerful in view of his circumstances. 'I woul'nt go any place else.'

Nowhere is evidence of the problems of the community served by Cook more acutely distressing than in the intensive-care unit of the hospital's obstetrics department, where babies born as early as the 28th week of pregnancy, and weighing as little as one-and-a-half pounds are cared for. Such births are usually the result of inadequate pre-natal care, poor diet, and possibly drug or alcohol abuse in a mother who may be in her early or mid-teens. Here, too, one learns that the greatest cause of death among expectant mothers in Chicago is not complications of pregnancy but gunshot wounds — the sort of alarming fact that doctors at Cook tend to drop without batting an eyelid.

(from *Radio Times*)

Exam comprehensions: a survival guide

A *Read the instructions and do only as much as you are asked to do!* For example:

If seven words are given and you are asked to give the meaning of five — do five only — even if you do seven only the first five will be marked.

B If you are asked to give the meaning of a word or phrase *give the exact equivalent*. For example:

- if the word is plural — such as 'commodities' give a plural equivalent — 'goods', or 'articles of trade'
- if the word is a noun — such as 'donor' give a noun equivalent — 'one who gives'.

C Don't use words you are asked to explain, in the explanation. For example:

- do *not* explain 'underprivileged areas' by 'these are *areas* . . .'
- do *not* explain 'pledging session' by 'this is a *session* where . . .'

D *Spelling.* At least spell correctly words given in the exam or question paper!

E Where it asks for the meaning of a word or phrase does it:
  (i) just ask that? — if so, a dictionary definition is acceptable, or
  (ii) say e.g. 'as used in the passage'? — if so, check that your alternative would fit in the passage — some words have several possible meanings, not all of which would be appropriate.

F Number your answers *exactly* as the question paper does — anything else may lose marks.

G The above simply require *concentration*.

Remember: carelessness costs marks!

Summary and precis writing

Only *the main points* of a passage are needed in a summary. Recognising the difference between main points and illustrative examples, anecdotes, 'padding' etc. is therefore a vital skill.

Once you have this skill writing within the number of words required is no longer a problem. Indeed, you may feel that you don't even need the number offered.

To take a rather exaggerated example read the following passage about the Peter Principle (which states that 'every employee tends to rise to his level of incompetence').

The Peter Principle: an introduction

As an author and journalist, I have had exceptional opportunities to study the workings of civilized society. I have investigated and written about government, industry, business, education and the arts. I have talked to, and listened carefully to, members of many trades and professions, people of lofty, middling and lowly stations.

I have noticed that, with few exceptions, men bungle their affairs. Everywhere I see incompetence rampant, incompetence triumphant.

I have seen a three-quarter-mile-long highway bridge collapse and fall into the sea because, despite checks and double-checks, someone had botched the design of a supporting pier.

I have seen town planners supervising the development of a city on the flood plain of a great river, where it is certain to be periodically inundated.

Lately I read about the collapse of three giant cooling towers at a British power-station: they cost a million dollars each, but were not strong enough to withstand a good blow of wind.

I noted with interest that the indoor baseball stadium at Houston, Texas, was found on completion to be peculiarly ill-suited to baseball: on bright days, fielders could not see fly balls against the glare of the skylights.

I observe that appliance manufacturers, as regular policy, establish regional service depots in the expectation — justified by experience — that many of their machines will break down during the warranty period.

Having listened to umpteen motorists' complaints about faults in their new cars, I was not surprised to learn that roughly one-fifth of the automobiles produced by major manufacturers in recent years have been found to contain potentially dangerous production defects.

Please do not assume that I am a jaundiced ultra-conservative, crying down contemporary men and things just because they are contemporary. Incompetence knows no barriers of time or place.

Macaulay gives a picture, drawn from a report by Samuel Pepys, of the British navy in 1648. 'The naval administration was a prodigy of wastefulness, corruption, ignorance, and indolence . . . no estimate could be trusted . . . no contract was performed . . . no check was enforced . . . Some of the new men of war were so rotten that, unless speedily repaired, they would go down at their moorings. The sailors were paid with so little punctuality that they were glad to find some usurer who would purchase their tickets at forty per cent discount. Most of the ships which were afloat were commanded by men who had not been bred to the sea.'

Wellington, examining the roster of officers assigned to him for the 1810 campaign in Portugal, said, 'I only hope that when the enemy reads the list of their names, he trembles as I do.'

Civil War General Richard Raylor, speaking of the Battle of the Seven Days, remarked, 'Confederate commanders knew no more about the topography ... within a day's march of the city of Richmond than they did about Central Africa.'

Robert E. Lee once complained bitterly, 'I cannot have my orders carried out.'

For most of World War II the British armed forces fought with explosives much inferior, weight for weight, to those in German shells and bombs. Early in 1940, British scientists knew that the cheap, simple addition of a little powdered aluminium would double the power of existing explosives, yet the knowledge was not applied till late in 1943.

In the same war, the Australian commander of a hospital ship checked the vessel's water tanks after a refit and found them painted inside with read lead. It would have poisoned every man aboard.

These things — and hundreds more like them — I have seen and read about and heard about. I have accepted the universality of incompetence.

(from *The Peter Principle* by L J Peter and R Hull)

There is really only one main point in this whole passage. As the writer says, 'men bungle their affairs'. The rest of the passage simply illustrates this point. Generally speaking each paragraph simply offers a fresh illustration.

A paragraph by paragraph analysis would go something like this:

1st paragraph. The writer's wide experience.
2nd paragraph. Leads him to believe 'men bungle their affairs'.
3rd–8th paragraphs. Modern examples of this.
9th paragraph. Not just a modern problem: happened in the past too.
10th–15th paragraphs. Historical examples of this.
16th paragraph. Leading to the conclusion — 'I have accepted the universality of incompetence'.

Now read the following passage:

Bones

Just how much sex is there in a skeleton? When archaeologists state categorically that half a femur comes from a twenty-year-old woman we are impressed with their certainty, not the less so because the statement, being a guess, is utterly unverifiable. Such a guess is as much based on the archaeologists' assumptions about women as anything else. What they mean is that the bone is typically female, that is, that it ought to belong to a woman. Because it is impossible to escape from the stereotyped notions of womanhood as they prevail in one's own society, curious errors in ascription have been made and continue to be made.

We tend to think of the skeleton as rigid; it seems to abide when all else withers away, so it ought to be a sort of nitty-gritty, unmarked by superficial conditioning. In fact it is itself subject to deformation by many influences. The first of these is muscular stress. Because men are

155

more vigorous than women their bones have more clearly marked muscular grooves. If the muscles are constrained, by binding or wasting, or by continual external pressure which is not counter-balanced, the bones can be drawn out of alignment. Men's bodies are altered by the work that they do, and by the nutriment which sustains them in their growing period, and so are women's, but women add to these influences others which are dictated by fashion and sex-appeal. There have been great changes in the history of feminine allure in the approved posture of the shoulders, whether sloping or straight, drawn forward or back, and these have been bolstered by dress and corsetting, so that the delicate balance of bone on bone has been altered by the stress of muscles maintaining the artificial posture. The spine has been curved forward in the mannequin's lope, or backwards in the S-bend of art nouveau or the sway-back of the fifties. Footwear reinforces these unnatural stresses; the high-heeled shoe alters all the torsion of the muscles of the thighs and pelvis and throws the spine into an angle which is still in some circles considered essential to allure. I am not so young that I cannot remember my grandmother begging my mother to corset me, because she found my teenage ungainliness unattractive, and was afraid that my back was not strong enough to maintain my height by itself. If I had been corseted at thirteen, my rib-cage might have developed differently, and the downward pressure on my pelvis would have resulted in its widening. Nowadays, corseting is frowned upon, but many women would not dream of casting away the girdle that offers support and tummy control. Even tights are tight, and can cause strange symptoms in the wearer. Typists' slouch and shop-girl lounge have their own effect upon the posture and therefore upon the skeleton.

Most people understand that the development of the limbs is affected by the exercise taken by the growing child. My mother discouraged us from emulating the famous girl swimmers of Australia by remarking on their massive shoulders and narrow hips, which she maintained came from their rigorous training. It is agreed that little girls should have a different physical education programme from little boys, but it is not admitted how much of the difference is counselled by the conviction that little girls should not look like little boys. The same assumptions extend into our suppositions about male and female skeletons: a small-handed skeleton ought to be female, small feet are feminine too, but the fact remains that either sex may exhibit the disproportion.

(from *The Female Eunuch* by Germaine Greer)

The first third of this passage contained developing argument and changing information. Even so we could probably summarise the first 238 words something like this:

When archaeologists tell us what sex a skeleton is they are working from a set idea of what a female skeleton *should* look like. Yet skeletons are not a fixed shape. Muscular stress is just one factor that affects their shape, and this stress can be created by the work people do or the fashions they wear. (*57 words*)

The next third (about 237 words) doesn't, however, so much add new ideas as illustrate the points already made. It could perhaps be summarised as:

Fashion changes, past and present, have affected, variously, the shoulders, back, spine, thighs and pelvis. *(15 words)*

The last paragraph does at least add a new point, which could be summarised thus:

It is not always recognised that the exercises children are encouraged to do are those which will produce the limb development considered appropriate for their sex. *(26 words)*

and clarifies an earlier point:

Ideas of what each sex *should* look like affect ideas of what sex skeletons are but don't *prove* that sex. *(20 words)*

Put the bracketed parts together, incidentally, and you have a 118 word summary of a 598 word passage, i.e. a summary about *one-fifth* the size of the original passage.

Notice some of the summary techniques used above.

- *More time was spent summarising the ideas* (e.g. in the first third of the passage) than the examples and illustrations (e.g. in the second third).

- *Generalisations replaced specific details* — e.g.

  that half a femur comes from a twenty-year-old woman

  became

  what sex a skeleton is

  and

  If the muscles are constrained, by binding or wasting, or by continued external pressure which is not counterbalanced, the bones can be drawn out of alignment

  became

  muscular stress . . . affects their shape.

- *Simple language replaced complicated* — e.g.

  the stereotyped notions of womanhood as they prevail in one's own society

  became

  set ideas about women.

Exercise

7.6

Look back at the passages for DIY Comprehension and try to summarise those you found most interesting. Aim to produce a summary no more than *one-third* the original length.

Taking notes

Note-taking is a useful skill. It is especially useful in offices and colleges. Whether you are taking a telephone message, preparing a report, or trying to sum up the main points of a book or a lesson, skill in note-taking will make your work easier. Here are some hints to improve your note-taking.

Concentrate on what you are reading or listening to. (The more you are distracted the more likely you are to confuse the message or to miss the main points.)

You don't need proper sentences. Use the shortest form you will still be able to understand when you read it again a few days or weeks or months later. For instance you may be able to miss out common words like *the* or *a*.

Abbreviate. Use your own abbreviations and shorthand, such as:

e.g. (for example), etc. (and so on), & (and), e.t.a. (estimated time of arrival), shd (should), wd (would), cd (could), v (very), info (information), > (becomes), < (comes from), 20 (twentieth century), ∴ (therefore), ≠ (does not equal).

However — in telephone messages — always write names, addresses, figures and difficult spellings out in full!

Main points only? Learn to recognise these — also to recognise what are just extra examples or points being repeated or words used for their own sake. Don't include more than you need — *concentrate on the essentials*! (Whether or not to include examples, and if so how many, will depend on your purpose. If, for instance, you are taking notes from a lesson to use in an essay you are writing then selected examples would be useful, as you would need them to substantiate the main points in the essay.)

Use headings and sub-headings

Use underlining and/or block capitals to emphasise headings

After making notes from a spoken message you may have to go back over the notes to do this — when listening to a message you will not always know what the speaker is going to say — so you will not always be sure exactly what the main points will be — once the speaker has finished you should have a clearer idea so will be able to look back and underline what was more important.

Rewriting? If the notes are to be used by someone else, you will probably need to rewrite them in order for them to be understandable. In that case you may decide to *change the order* of the notes, should that make more sense.

Read this passage and consider what notes should be taken:

Ideals of feminine beauty seem to swing backwards and forwards between the mobile and the static, between the expressive and the inexpressive. Egyptian civilisation was probably the first to represent a woman we should call beautiful today; and the Egyptians, it is clear from their portrait-heads and wall-paintings, preferred extremely animated women. The celebrated head of Queen Nefertiti, now at Berlin, has become a little too familiar; but an unfinished head in the Cairo Museum still surprises and delights us; and pictures of fashionable ladies about 1450 BC listening to music, drinking wine, and occasionally, being sick at parties, show the worldly lives they led.

Elsewhere, in other countries and periods of civilisation, the least animated faces have seemed the most compelling. Thus, in Japanese art, beautiful women are always represented as utterly expressionless; and when Utamaro immortalised the well-known beauties of 'the Floating World', the world of courtesans and their retainers, he dwelt on the practised elegance with which they executed some simple action, rather than on their individual faces. Those faces, far from revealing a separate personality, resembled abstract works of art, eyebrows shaved off and replaced by neatly painted crescent moon, complexions smothered in wet-white, eyes narrowed to slits and teeth unkindly blackened. Many of Utamaro's prints depict extravagant erotic scenes; but even there, the woman's coiffure is seldom disarrayed and her expression never changes.

(from *Sunday Times Magazine* 1977)

In this passage the main point — that there have always been two contrasting ideals of female beauty, the expressive and the expressionless — is made in the first sentence. The rest of the two paragraphs consists of detail about two contrasting examples; how much we choose to include in notes would depend on what we wanted the notes for, and how much time was available. We could produce as little as this:

Feminine Beauty

(A)　　2 contrasting ideals through the ages:
(1) *Expressive,* e.g. Ancient Egypt (Queen Nefertiti etc.)
(2) *Expressionless,* e.g. Japan (even in Utamaro's erotic paintings)

What, if anything, would you add to these notes? And why?

Exercise 7.7

Make notes on the following passages. (Assume you are collecting material for a project on 'The Beauty Industry')

(a) Perfume started life as an incense burned in temples (perfume, in Latin, means literally 'through smoke'). The Greeks and Romans drenched themselves, their horses and their dogs in it and Cleopatra went to meet Antony in a scent-soaked barge. But it didn't become a vast commercial proposition until the 1920s and 1930s when the Haute Couture, spearheaded by Chanel and Lanvin moved in. This was when synthetic ingredients were used for the first time; it would have been impossible to make Chanel No. 5 without them. (Why No. 5? Chanel chose it from a test bottle labelled No. 5, that's all.) British couture houses were slow to follow — finally in 1953 Hartnell launched In Love, sweet, slightly cloying, romantic, and still a great seller in Scotland . . .

There's a big divide between American and French perfumes. American scents are knock-out blows — "women in the States like to smell perfume on themselves, while European women wear it more subtly for other people to smell" said a European expert. "One American scent can be sussed out at 50 paces . . ."

There are two ways of selling scent: the way the classic houses do it, slowly building up a market to last, keeping supplies limited to the better shops; or the American cosmetic-house operation, heavily backed by advertising, where if a perfume doesn't make it within 18 months, it is quietly taken off the market. The promoted scents brought in new young customers who don't want a 'signature' scent of their own, but often use four or five.

Revlon's Charlie was one of the first of the promoted perfumes, and began a range of scents with a sporty unisex image; a batch of 'liberated' perfume came in with butch names like Charlie, and Coty's Smitty. At the same time men were being assailed by Ha'i Karate and, of course, Brut. "The Charlies, the younger cheaper perfumes, have done nothing but good," says Chanel. "They've made young people aware of perfume; after that they go on to French fragrance as they become more knowledgeable, rather like wine drinkers."

(from *Sunday Times Magazine* 1977)

(b) Ever since caveman stopped clubbing cavewoman, the art of seduction has depended at least a little on a man's attractiveness to a woman. Today even mascara on male eyelashes is no longer tantamount to Sodom and Gomorrah and the Fall of the Roman Empire. And the use of a little lip gloss doesn't mean you're a poof.

More than one politician has seen fit to rebut such allegations. Exactly 100 years ago, Disraeli was moved to note: "The two most manly persons I ever knew, Palmerston and Lyndhurst, both rouged. So one must not trust too much to general observation."

The hidden persuaders of the advertising world have still had some trouble getting most men to do much to protect or enhance their beauty with products and treatments. Men perhaps remain a little guilty about caring.

Even deodorants prove too much for some citizens who believe in the simple virtues of carbolic soap and a scrubbing brush. Dr. Beric Wright, medical advisor to the Institute of Directors, has described the smell of commuters as "the sort I imagine you get in a Turkish Brothel".

Dr. Wright's point is that men are conned into buying unnecessarily expensive cosmetics. That they can be expensive is beyond dispute. A set of the 16 Aramis 900 products, for instance, costs more than £60 and is pretentiously described as 'grooming formulae ... interrelated scientifically to cope with the total man". Whoever total man is he does respond. It is expensive male products (cosmetics) that are enjoying increased sales. An Aramis spokesman says: "People like to pamper themselves. It consoles them. We are thinking of a new, even more expensive range."

The fully made-up male face still seems restricted to the stage, film and advertising studios. Regis, a make-up artist who has painted Mick Jagger's features, says, "Most rock stars now wear much less make-up even on stage — except of course for punks . . ."

Men are more concerned about hair than about any other aspect of their appearance. They spend a lot of time getting rid of it from their faces and rather more time worrying about losing it from their heads. The £7.5 m spent by men last year on sprays, shampoos, dyes, tonics, conditioners and colour rinses bears witness to a vanity which for no good scientific reason equates going bald with the onset of impotence. In fact the only way of stopping premature baldness is castration — about the one thing men seem loath to try.

(from *Sunday Times Magazine* 1977)

Some final comprehension practice

Read the following passage and answer the questions which follow.

Exercise

7.8

Tongue-tied by too much TV!

An elaborate four-year study of 350 American families has come up with some disturbing news about the effect of television viewing on the reading and speaking skills of children.

It finds that by the age of six, real differences appear between children who watch TV for three hours or more a day and those who watch for one hour or less. The heavy viewers are more likely to be retarded in reading and comprehension and limited in their conversational range, using fewer adjectives and adverbs and shorter, simpler sentences.

Television also affects their ability to imagine and share possessions and experiences with other children.

Devised by a husband and wife team of psychologists, Jerome and Dorothy Singer, at Yale University's family television research programme, the study is extraordinary in that it monitored selected families continuously and closely for four years, unlike most others which are confined to a period of a few weeks under laboratory conditions.

The results, hot off the Yale computers are more dismaying than expected. "The idea that TV affects reading, language and comprehension is not just conjecture," Dorothy Singer said. "Now we know for certain that this is so. What the study tells us is that watching TV is not enough to give a child a vocabulary. Unless words are used in their own experience and reinforced with play the words will not be internalised."

In the course of their research the Singers have made some important discoveries. One is that reading is a much more complex mental skill than might be supposed. Young children need to look at picture books and use their imagination actively BEFORE they start learning to read. They must be encouraged to invent their own world of make-believe, playing with model villages, imitating the voices of fantasy characters, having space-travel adventures in their minds.

"When a child plays he cuts the world down to size," Jerome Singer said. "The world is a big, complicated place, and play puts it under his own power. He can manipulate, change and rearrange it. This has an important effect on his ability to master printed material later on, when he needs to be aware that stories have a beginning, a middle and an end. Watching television is too passive for this purpose."

The Singers also found that children whose parents read to them and tell them stories in infancy are most likely to be able to resist the temptations of TV later in childhood. The viewing habits of parents are a key indicator of the future viewing habits of their children.

Certain types of TV programmes have worse effects on children than others. Cartoons make them less enthusiastic about learning, and more aggressive, pushing and shoving other children.

Shows containing a great deal of action, calculated to hold the viewer's eye to the screen and keep him watching when the commercials come on, tend to induce destructive behaviour in these youngsters leading them to damage property.

A number of worrying facts arise from this remarkably thorough Yale study. Children who are heavy viewers have become the norm rather than the exception in America. Pre-schoolers watch television for three and a half hours a day, on the average. By the age of 11 or 12 they are glued to the screen for between four and a half and five hours a day.

That means that light-viewing children around the age of six, the ones who tend to be better readers, use more advanced vocabularies and speak complete sentences, are a minority. And six is a crucial age, when a child either begins to acquire knowledge at a rapid rate or drifts towards the sidelines, setting a pattern for the rest of his school years.

"We have almost given up hope of changing children's TV addiction," Mr Singer said "We have talked to parents and urged them to reduce the amount of time their children spend watching TV, but with no success. Television is too much built into the fabric of daily life. It's too convenient.

The best we can do now is to teach children at school about the nature of the television medium, how commercials are made, the limited scope of news and the fact that aggressive behaviour on the screen is carefully staged, using actors and actresses. Most children are under the impression that it's all real."

(from *The New Standard* 1981)

1)   In what ways did the Singers' research differ from previous studies?

2)   Why is watching TV not enough to give a child a vocabulary?

3) In your own words explain the importance of play for a child's development.

4) Which types of TV programmes are specifically referred to as having harmful effects on children's behaviour?

5) Choose any *four* of the following and suggest a word or phrase which could replace each in the passage:

    (i)   *retarded*   (paragraph 2)

    (ii) *monitored*   (paragraph 4)

    (iii) *conjecture*   (paragraph 5)

    (iv) *internalised* (paragraph 5)

    (v) *manipulate*   (paragraph 7)

    (vi) *induce*   (paragraph 10)

    (vii) *acquire*   (paragraph 12)

6) In not more than 30 words summarise the harmful effects of heavy TV viewing upon children, according to the passage.

7) If you had written this passage would you have used phrases like *hot off the Yale computers* and *glued to the screen*? Explain why/why not.

8) Using the information in the passage how could you reduce the harmful effects of television viewing on children

    (i) as a parent?

    (ii) as a teacher?

9) While researching a project on language development in children you discover this article. Make short, *selective* notes on the passage, suitable for this purpose.

10) Do you find the article convincing in its account of how TV viewing affects children? Explain why/why not.

Exercise 7.9

Read the following passage and answer the questions which follow.

Spare the rules, spoil the child

A child is sometimes the most susceptible and vulnerable consumer of all. Which is why any advertising aimed at children needs tight control. Hence the rules below.

Appendix B: Children

General

1.1 Direct appeals or exhortations to buy should not be made to children unless the product advertised is one likely to be of interest to them which they could reasonably be expected to afford for themselves.

1.2 Advertisements should not encourage children to make themselves a nuisance to their parents, or anyone else, with the aim of persuading them to buy an advertised product.

1.3 No advertisement should cause children to believe that they will be inferior to other children, or unpopular with them, if they do not buy a particular product, or have it bought for them.

1.4 No advertisement for a commercial product should suggest to children that, if they do not buy it or encourage others to do so, they will be failing in their duty or lacking in loyalty.

1.5 Advertisements addressed to children should make it easy for a child to judge the true size of a product (preferably by showing it in relation to some common object) and should take care to avoid any confusion between the characteristics of real-life articles and toy copies of them.

1.6 Where the results obtainable by the use of a product are shown, these should not exaggerate what is attainable by an ordinary child.

1.7 Advertisements addressed to children should wherever possible give the price of the advertised product.

Safety

2.1 No advertisement, particularly for a collecting scheme, should encourage children to enter strange places or to converse with strangers in an effort to collect coupons, wrappers, labels or the like.

2.2 Children should not appear to be unattended in street scenes unless they are obviously old enough to be responsible for their own safety; should not be shown playing in the road, unless it is clearly shown to be a play street or other safe area; should not be shown stepping carelessly off the pavement or crossing the road without due care; in busy street scenes should be seen to use the zebra crossings when crossing the road; and should be otherwise seen in general, as pedestrians or cyclists, to behave in accord-with the Highway Code.

2.3 . . .

These are just some of the rules affecting children's advertising and they appear in a book called the *British Code of Advertising Practice.* In it are many rules, not just affecting children's advertising. They govern all advertisements which appear in the press, or in direct mail, in print, on posters and cinema commercials.

The Code is used by the Advertising Standards Authority whose job it is to protect the public from unacceptable advertising. (To help us interpret and develop the Code, we have recently carried out research into children's reactions to advertisements.)

Amongst other things, the ASA responds to consumers' complaints, and this briefly is the way the system works. Members of the public can write to us to complain about any advertisement they find unacceptable. If, after investigation, we find the advertisement contravenes the Code, we instruct the advertiser to amend or withdraw the advertisement.

If you would like to know more about the Code on advertisements addressed to children, or about us, or if you have any cause to complain about an advertisement, we'd like to hear from you.

If an advertiser breaks one of the rules, we won't let him get off lightly.

THE ADVERTISING STANDARDS AUTHORITY
If an advertisement is wrong, we're here to put it right.

(from The Advertising Standards Authority advertisement in *The Times Educational Supplement* 1981)

1) Take point 1.1 and suggest a specific article which *could* be advertised by 'direct appeals or exhortations'. Explain why.

2) Design an advertisement for a toy watch which conforms to rules 1.5 and 1.7.

3) Suggest *three* more rules for advertisements for children.

4) In not more than 90 words summarise Appendix B, points 1.1 to 1.7 (General).

5) Choose any *three* of the following and suggest a word or phrase which could replace each in the passage:

   (i)   *susceptible*   (paragraph 1)

   (ii) *vulnerable*   (paragraph 1)

   (iii) *exhortations* (section 1.1)

   (iv) *attainable*   (section 1.6)

   (v)   *interpret*   (paragraph 3)

   (vi) *contravenes*   (paragraph 4)

6) What is the ASA?

7) What does the ASA do?

8) Are there any advertisements which do not appear to be covered by the British Code of Advertising Practice?

9) From what you have read in the passage do you believe the ASA is doing a good job? Explain why/why not.

The end?

Although this is the end of the book, I hope it won't be the end of your interest in English. A lot of sections in the book are worth following up further — as are many of the extracts. Good luck with your present English course, and in any English examinations you are due to take.